SHAPING A SERVANT LEADER

Neville Ying

outskirts press

Shaping a Servant Leader
All Rights Reserved.
Copyright © 2021 Neville Ying
v1.0

The opinions expressed in this manuscript are solely the opinions of the author and do not represent the opinions or thoughts of the publisher. The author has represented and warranted full ownership and/or legal right to publish all the materials in this book.

This book may not be reproduced, transmitted, or stored in whole or in part by any means, including graphic, electronic, or mechanical without the express written consent of the publisher except in the case of brief quotations embodied in critical articles and reviews.

Outskirts Press, Inc.
http://www.outskirtspress.com

Paperback ISBN: 978-1-9772-4045-3
Hardback ISBN: 978-1-9772-4046-0

Cover Photo © 2021 Christopher Samuels. All rights reserved - used with permission.
Manuscript Development: Glynis Salmon
Copy Editing: Outskirts Press

Outskirts Press and the "OP" logo are trademarks belonging to Outskirts Press, Inc.

PRINTED IN THE UNITED STATES OF AMERICA

Contents

Dedication i

Acknowledgments iv

Invitation to Read ix

Preface

Part 1: Prepping the Clay x

Part 2: Centering the Clay xx

Introduction.. xxix

1. Raising Up the Servant Leader:
   Stories, Lessons, and Impact of Childhood Experiences 1

2. Growing Up the Servant Leader:
   Stories, Lessons, and Impact of Boyhood Experiences 21

3. Schooling the Servant Leader:
   Stories, Lessons, and Impact of Elementary Schooling............ 29

It is their generous (and dare I say, mutually rewarding) support that has enabled many of the stories that are liberally placed throughout this book to have come to light. We laughed uproariously and reveled in the recall of many of them, and sobered at the treasure trove of lessons learnt.

Thank you Lascelles Dixon, Lloyd Delpratt, C. K. Robinson, Rudolph Daley, Conrad Francis, and Stanley Tracey (Dinthill); Horace Lewis, Class of 1959; Vivian Crawford, Owen James, Albert Neufville, Class of 1962; Walter Subadan and Henry Sterling, Class of 1961(The Mico); Lilieth Nelson, Ronnie Young, and the late Willard Pinnock, Class of 1967 (University of the West Indies, UWI); Karl Wright (University of Maryland, UM); Leo Gooden and Eric Budhlall (Ministry of Education); Silvera Castro (St. Andrew Technical High School (STATHS). I deeply value and appreciate your friendship, assistance with fact checks, sharing of memories, and unwavering support.

My profound and special thanks to Glynis Salmon, Bala Press, who provided professional expertise, guidance, and support for manuscript development.

Special thanks to Cristopher Samuels for his professional artistic expertise on the design of the front and back covers of the book and the copy editor, Outskirts Press, for the meticulous and professional editorial review which added value to the quality of the manuscript.

You, together with my friends, family members, and fellow travelers in my sojourn through elementary school, high school, college, universities, and my early working career have collaborated with me to shape this book into a creative and worthwhile piece.

Acknowledgments

In writing this book I had to reflect on the experiences that shaped me as a servant leader, from elementary school, high school, and studies at institutions of higher learning to my early working career. This was a long period of time so I needed help.

Basil McCalla, who provided me with information from our elementary school days, pointed out to me that as we get older, we still have vast amounts of information stored in our "mental computer." It is, however, the "retrieval process" that takes longer! I concur.

He was quick to remind me that this truism was shared with him by my great friend, school and college mate, the late David Telfer.

Well, I did need some help with the retrieval of the rich cache of stories culled from my life's journey and stored in my mental computer.

I am indebted to the generous support of some of my special "journey" companions from the world of education and work, who joined me in the process of retrieving the memories and/or fact checking, and making sense of the experiences.

"present-continuous," with ever-multiplying and mutually rewarding benefits. May your reading of this book further shape and sharpen your servant leadership character.

It is to God that I reserve my highest praise and honour, for it is His light that guides my servant leadership.

to live purposefully and make a positive difference in their own and other's lives.

The headmaster of my elementary school (Morant Bay Elementary School, St. Thomas, Jamaica), the late D.R.B. Grant, and my class teacher, the late Conex Jarrett, both raised the structure from my early foundation of home training and enabled me to rise and express my full potential as a young scholar and well-rounded youth leader. It is their confidence in my abilities, their care to nurture and mentor, and their wisdom to point and guide me in the right direction that has led me to experience a high level of personal and professional success and quality of service to people and organizations.

The love and support of family is invaluable. They are the true keepers of the faith, and so much more! I am eternally grateful for the amazing gift of my family, immediate and extended, who have been a tower of strength, guidance, support, encouragement, and inspiration at different points throughout my life.

My dear wife, Esther, provided me with the love, psychological support, and encouragement while I developed and honed my servant leadership skills and competences.

My wonderful children presented me with the opportunity to experiment and practice one of the most important features of servant leadership: *empowerment*—to assist persons to be the best that they can be and do their best in all they do.

All my friends, colleagues, and others who have peopled my world, and who have enriched my life and my servant leadership character with their presence and contribution.

To all who read this book, especially the youth and all emerging and established servant leaders, the journey of service to others is

Dedication

Writing a book is a wonderful though grueling process. Now that it is completed, I am faced with the further challenge of dedicating this work to one or a group of persons who have most impacted my life and contributed significantly to shaping me as a servant leader.

The truth is, all who have crossed my path on my journey through life have left a positive imprint of experience, exposure, lessons, and insights, which have, in one way or another, served to shape my servant leadership character.

While there are many persons who have provided me with endless reasons why they have earned the distinction of being the subject of my dedication, the conventions of book dedications require that I limit my list and elevate to a place of honour, the persons to whom the highest recognition is due.

My late mother, through her practical demonstration of *faith, hope,* and *love,* taught me ethical principles and the importance of serving and empowering other persons. My mother empowered and enabled people to "rise" and "shine" and give full expression to their capacity

4. Developing the Servant Leader:
   Stories, Lessons, and Impact of the High School Years............. 39

5. Empowering the Servant Leader:
   Stories, Lessons, and Impact of the Collegiate Level 57

6. Advancing the Servant Leader:
   Stories, Lessons, and Impact of University
   and Continued Higher Learning 93

7. Employing the Servant Leader:
   Stories, Lessons, and Impact of the World of Work:
   Teaching and Administration 137

8. The Servant Leader Ready for Service:
   Lessons Learnt, Competencies Acquired, Insights Gained 168

Conclusion: Shaping a Servant Leader: A Continuous Process 183

7/2021

A servant leader is one who provides leadership by establishing and nurturing relationships with people with the priority intention of empowering them to have the capacity and passion to improve the quality of their lives. —

Invitation to Read

Join me as I undertake a process of personal introspection and reflection on my journey through life. Along the way, I will share some of the experiences and exposures I encountered that shaped me as a leader and more specifically, as a servant leader.

Neville Ying

Preface
Part 1: Prepping the Clay

The concept of "servant" as "leader" is not new. It is an approach that has been used from time immemorial.

It is a concept that is rooted in ancient philosophy, with advocates such as Lao Tzu (philosopher of ancient China) and Chanakya (philosopher, teacher, and economist of ancient India).

Mother Teresa (honoured in the Catholic Church as a saint) and Mahatma Gandhi (anticolonial nationalist and political ethicist), were among those who established themselves as servant leaders.

Jesus's washing of his disciple's feet and his entire life and teachings of love, humility, and service to others are a model of servant leadership.

There are so many examples in history and in religion that point to the advocacy and practice of servant leadership.

It was Robert Greenleaf, however, who is credited with first coining and popularizing the term "servant leadership." He wrote it in an essay that he later expanded into a book. He capsulized his views and perspectives on servant leadership in the following statement:

As a servant-leader you're 'a servant first' – you focus on the needs of others especially team members, before you consider your own.

Servant leadership is less about a leadership style or technique, and more about a "way of being" that has been influenced, developed, and/or cultivated over time.

It may even be described as a philosophy or a set of practices that focus on the needs, well-being, growth, and development of others, and seeks to *inspire*, *empower*, *enrich*, and *transform* to achieve optimum performance outcomes and impact.

The servant leader, against the background of an organizational setting, is first and foremost a servant—serving others with respect and humility, acknowledging their perspectives, providing support to meet their goals, facilitating input in decision-making, building a strong sense of community, and strengthening internal and external stakeholder trust, pride, engagement, innovation, and productivity.

On the other hand, in the same organizational setting, the leader, in its more traditional expression, focuses on productivity and performance outcomes first, with relatively less regard for persons beyond their being a "means to an end"…forgetting that it is inspired, motivated, and empowered people with their creative ideas and innovative actions that really make an organization productive, successful, and sustainable.

Servant leadership is not a costume to be put on or taken off as the leadership role dictates. It is an authentic "being-ness," woven from a conscious choice to serve the needs of others, to respect and amplify their value, and to enable them to unleash their full potential.

Nor is servant leadership an overnight affair. It is an ever-evolving process of developing and nurturing a sound and solid servant leadership character.

It is a "service mindset" that creates strong and mutually rewarding relationships, and a commitment to enabling others to achieve the best possible results. It is a choice to be empathetic and connect with people, and prioritize their needs over self.

In consonance with this I have developed my own view about who is a servant leader, stated as follows:

> A servant leader is one who provides leadership by establishing and nurturing relationships with people with the priority intention of empowering them to have the capacity and passion to improve the quality of their lives.

Servant leadership expert, Larry C. Spears, president and CEO of the Greenleaf Center for Servant-Leadership, writes in *Servant Leadership in Action*:

> Servant leadership characteristics often occur naturally within many individuals and, like many natural tendencies, they can be enhanced through learning and practice.

Spears identifies the ten most common servant leadership characteristics as:

- listening,
- empathy,

- healing,
- awareness,
- persuasion,
- conceptualization
- foresight,
- stewardship,
- commitment to others' growth, and
- community building.

Regrettably, many leaders are not inspired or encouraged to develop and demonstrate these characteristics. As a result, their visioning for the future, and its implementation, falls strategically short; hence, the impact of their leadership is limited.

In today's world, one of the most frequently used words is "leadership." Yet, though widely used and applied to leaders at all levels in diverse spheres of interest, it is a word not fully understood (or clearly defined for that matter), and correspondingly, not well understood or practiced.

In this new era of leadership, leaders across the globe are engaged in the process of trying to make a difference and effecting profound changes in their respective areas of influence. Each leader wants to be effective, impactful, and transformative.

But how can leaders achieve this?

Do they understand what it takes to be an effective leader?

Are they more concerned with themselves and their status as a leader than with the role of being a leader?

Are they more taken with their achievements, their power, and their authority, or with the development and empowerment of others?

The questions could go on and on, and lead us into deep examination of leadership and the characteristics of a leader.

Leadership and, in particular, servant leadership is a compelling issue and demands all due attention and interrogation of these fundamental questions. Perhaps, though, it would be best if we start at the very beginning, with the fundamental question:

Who are leaders and what are their attributes?

Leaders don't all come from the same background or follow the same path. Each leader brings his/her perspective and/or definition of leadership, which influences how they lead.

Every leader has his or her own vision and direction. Leadership styles and approaches change as the leaders and other influencing factors change.

So you may well ask, "What makes a leader a leader?"

In attempting to answer this question, another perhaps even more fundamental question needs to be asked: "What shaped the leadership attributes leaders demonstrate?"

This question brings into sharp focus, the age-old Nature vs. Nurture debate.

In the context of leadership and leaders in this debate, the critical questions would be:

Are some persons born with the propensity and capability to be leaders?

Are leadership competencies acquired over time through a combination of training and cumulative experiences?

In advancing the debate, I decided to put forward my response to these questions in this book.

I invite you to join me as I undertake a process of personal introspection and reflection on my journey through life. Along the way, I will share some of the experiences and exposures I encountered that I believe shaped me as a leader and, more specifically, as a *servant leader*.

In deciding to write this book, I also determined that I would use a particular approach in writing it. This approach was concretized as a result of the following circumstance:

Within a two-year span, 2018–2019, I received five prestigious awards in recognition and appreciation of my leadership and service contribution to advancing public service excellence and building institutional capacity.

Those awards expanded the cache of honours and awards that I had received over the years, including national honours and a building named in my honour.

Amid their applause and commendations, many of my friends and professional colleagues, some of whom I have known for over fifty years, in some dismay, commented, "I did not know that you were involved in so many things over the years!"

Some of these people also asked me, "What motivated you to give so many years of public service?"

As I reflected on my life, I realized the path that I travelled was richly strewn with many profound experiences and lessons that have undoubtedly shaped me as a servant leader.

I determined, therefore, that I had a responsibility and a duty of care as a leader to share the stories of my life's experiences and the wealth of lessons learnt with others.

This is especially so for our youth, leaders in different organizations who are working toward making a transformative difference, and individuals preparing for key leadership positions. These people may find something of value with which to build and/or strengthen their own servant leadership capacity.

I am a strong advocate of the value and importance of stories—the good, the bad, the ugly, and the seemingly indifferent. Stories drawn from one's life, from childhood onward, help persons to become more self-aware, teach leadership lessons, and influence leadership characteristics.

It is through our own life experiences that we become fully aware of our strengths and weaknesses and the factors that enabled our growth and development.

It is the stories that we share and the lived experience of the lessons learnt, more than any other factors, that are able to effectively influence self-awareness.

Self-awareness is one of the most critical factors in shaping a servant leader. Courtney E. Ackerman, a highly respected researcher, published author, and prolific writer for PositivePsychology.com, describes self-awareness as "the ability to see yourself clearly and objectively through reflection and introspection."

Life stories are therefore invaluable and should not be kept hidden. It is precisely because I am seized of that truth that I purposed to write this book and freely share with you some of my life stories, as well as those of others. It is my intention to connect the stories as they unfold, with key leadership lessons learnt.

The story of one of the many unique cultural practices of the *Inuits* or Eskimos—the aboriginal people who make their homes in the Arctic and subarctic regions of Siberia and North America—may best illustrate why I am compelled to write and share this book with you.

As the Inuits travelled in the extreme climatic conditions, one of the essential skills they developed for arctic survival was the construction of an *inuksuk*, a stone structure in which the Inuits stored food or tools for those journeying behind them and might need it.

There were times when the Inuits would build a chain of inuksuks. These were strategically located in a line and in such a way that travelers who might follow could see beyond the one they were standing beside to the next one off in the distance.

This strategic placement of the structures would prevent the travelers who followed from getting lost, particularly in extremely bad weather.

Such a traveler would be immeasurably grateful for the construct and placement of the sculpted stone markers along the way, and the thoughtful gift of food and tools that was left for them.

As with the practice of the Inuit traveler, and as a servant leader, I have built my own "inuksuk book," filled with food for thought and a toolkit of lessons, for young leaders and other travelers along the path of leadership, who could benefit from my contribution to the success of their onward journey.

This is my inuksuk book, which is constructed to facilitate ease of navigation through the stories and lessons. The path is strategically laid out, chapter by chapter, in a clear, simple, cohesive, and coherent way. It facilitates reflection and connection with many insights and truths to empower the leader-traveler's journey in a dynamic and ever-evolving leadership landscape.

I have endeavoured to present an open and honest narrative of experiences and events and those who peopled my world at different stages of my life.

I have placed particular emphasis on how these experiences, exposures, and persons, by their influence and impact, shaped me as a servant leader with the desire and drive for service.

It is my hope that my life's journey, the stories and lessons I share, will be especially relevant and valuable to all who read this book, in particular our young people.

I urge young people, especially those who may be experiencing seemingly "adverse" social and economic challenges or hardships, to stride purposefully onward, though beset by myriad obstacles. I urge them to rise above and move forward and onward toward success, in spite of seemingly debilitating circumstances.

The "rock-stone-hard" and harsh realities you may have encountered and the seemingly adverse experiences, when positioned in a positive and enlightened perspective, are but building blocks with which to build a solid platform, and from which to raise your construct of self-confidence, fixity of purpose, innovation, productivity, and success.

For those who are seasoned in leadership and currently occupy leadership positions, and for those who are positioning themselves to serve as leaders, it is my hope that my journey will inspire reflection on your own life's journey to date and lead you to mindfulness of the value and impact of holistic development on the quality of your life, service, and leadership.

> I don't know what your destiny will be, but one thing I do know: the only ones among you who will be really happy are those who have sought and found how to serve.—Albert Schweitzer

> When you choose the paradigm of service, looking at life through that paradigm, it turns everything you do from a job into a gift.—Oprah Winfrey

Preface
Part 2: Centering the Clay

> Telling stories is one of the most powerful means
> that leaders have to influence, teach, and inspire.
> We communicate through stories and learn from them...
> The stories help solidify relationships.
> —Vanessa Boris

I have carefully crafted this book as a compilation of strategically placed real-life stories.

Over the years I have found storytelling to be very effective in capturing the reader's/listener's attention, maintaining their interest and engagement, conveying meaning, and enabling connection.

In choosing to harvest and share with you some of the life stories that shaped me as a servant leader, I am minded to recall the memory of the late Sir Phillip Sherlock, former vice chancellor of the University of the West Indies (UWI), who greatly influenced my use of the storytelling approach for this book.

Sir Phillip was an impressive figure. He was a remarkable Caribbean scholar and educator, whose brilliant mind, generosity of spirit, and sterling contribution to nation building was an inspiration to generations.

I had the good fortune of meeting this great leader in the formative period of my youth, when everything was fresh and new and carried a powerful impact as I entered the hallowed halls of academia at the University of the West Indies. Forever etched in my mind is one of the stories Sir Phillip Sherlock told at my matriculation ceremony.

As the story goes…

A young man from the twin-island Republic of Trinidad and Tobago (TT) came to study at the Mona Campus. After three months, his girlfriend from TT wrote to him asking the following question:

"What do the girls in Jamaica have that I don't have?"

He sent her the following reply:

"The girls in Jamaica don't have anything you don't have! They just have it right here."

I do not remember the rest of Sir Phillip's matriculation address, but his story stuck in my mind. I never forgot it in my interaction with fellow students from other Caribbean (now CARICOM) countries outside of Jamaica.

Sir Phillip's use of storytelling to engage an audience and convey meaning impacted me greatly. Since then, I have emulated his communication style by incorporating stories in my presentations and engagement with others.

One year, when I taught a master's in business administration (MBA) class on transformational leadership, I gave my students a lunchtime assignment to read a chapter from the course textbook.

After lunch, one member of the class gave what the class thought was an impressive review and report of the assigned chapter. The class was eager to hear what they anticipated would be a very favourable response from me.

To their utter dismay, my response was "I can see that the class did a good job reading the summary at the end, and not the full chapter."

The class was quite bewildered by my response and asked me how I knew that they had read *only* the summary of the prescribed chapter, so I told them the following story:

During my first year in teachers' college, our class was given an assignment to read the Charles Dickens classic literary work *Great Expectations*.

I got around to reading only up to chapter 2 of the book. Then came the midterm test, with a question that required a discussion of a quotation from the book: "Hold me, I am so frightened!"

My response was "Pip was in the graveyard with Joe, and when the convict appeared, he said to Joe, 'Hold me, I am so frightened!'"

From my unfinished reading of the work, and my even more limited understanding of the story, my made-up answer to the question sounded good enough to me…even brilliant!

As it turned out, had I exerted myself to complete the reading of the book, I would have known that the quotation came from a much later section of the book. It was an exclamation made by Trabb's boy (assistant to Mr. Trabb) and not at all by Pip as I had incorrectly guessed.

My literature teacher laughed until tears flowed from her eyes when she read my answer to the class. I was then given the assignment to complete the reading of the entire book over the weekend and re-sit the test the next Monday morning.

In making the class aware that I knew they had short-changed themselves and the process by only reading the chapter summary, and not the entire chapter, I sought to convey to them, through the story, that I was quite "experienced" in the ways of students answering questions without completing the requisite reading.

Needless to say, I made them suffer, as I did umpteen years ago, the unerring principle of "cause and effect." They were all required to read the entire chapter in readiness for a test that I gave them in the next class. I believe they learnt their lesson well.

In one of my lectures on emotional intelligence competencies, I told the following story:

Once I had an interview with a lady who had applied for a senior manager's position. From the outset her body language signalled that she was distraught and decidedly uncomfortable.

I was sufficiently moved to dispense with the usual interview posture, and in a kind voice and tone, I put her at ease and engaged her in conversation.

"How are you feeling today?" was my opening enquiry.

Her response was immediate and unhesitating, as if she could not contain her pent-up distress one minute longer and welcomed the opportunity to unburden and release. She gushed out her story as follows:

"For the past five years my life has followed a certain routine. Each morning I take my daughter to school and then get to work on time. At lunchtime I pick up my daughter from school, take her home, and return to work to complete my assignments for the day. This morning when I arrived at work, I saw a pink slip on my desk, which served as a notice that my services are being terminated..."

I listened to her attentively, without interruption, and when she was through, our conversation flowed easily into becoming more of a counselling session and less of a job interview.

At the end of our discussion, she left refreshed, renewed, fortified, and empowered with fresh, new perspectives and a toolbox of self-awareness and self-management skills going forward.

In the process I was able to glean from our conversation all of the information I needed to assess her suitability for the position she sought in the organization. And yes, she did get the job!

Her performance value to the team and the organization was immeasurable. She has never ceased to remind me of how my response to her that day, under the circumstances, positively impacted her life and the character of her leadership.

In whatever sphere of life and endeavour I find myself, regardless of position influence or authority, I am *human* first.

It is that strong sense of my humanity and my "oneness" with others that underpin all my relationships and define my leadership.

The two cannot be separated—my leadership from my humanity.

When that young lady walked into my office to honour the scheduled job interview, and I sensed, rather than saw, her distress, it was my *humanness* that immediately came to the fore. In that moment, what mattered most was not the interview but rather, an "in" into where she was "at."

The offer of a listening ear, an empathetic response, and the possibility for renewal of the mind and spirit was, in that moment, far more valuable than my time to me or her need for a job to her. We were just two human beings sharing together.

What makes a leader? That is the eternal and universal question.

What makes a servant leader? That has now become the subject of ongoing enquiry and debate.

Simon Sinek, the British-born, American author and motivational speaker, answers both questions well: "If your actions inspire others to dream more, learn more, do more and become more, you are a leader."

It would seem then that Sinek's response implies that an authentic leader must have a heart of service to others in order to qualify as a leader. To do otherwise is to diminish the role and impact of leadership.

Robert Greenleaf, the founding inspirational leader of the servant leadership philosophy says, "The servant-leader is servant first...It begins with the natural feeling that one wants to serve, to serve first. Then conscious choice brings one to aspire to lead."

Leaders must see people first. Servants must see service first.

Servant leadership must come from the heart. It must foster inclusivity and inspiration, and right relationship with others. It is the key to unlocking and unleashing the full power and potential of individuals, teams, organizations, and communities.

So what shaped my servant leadership sensibilities? Everything!

From childhood onward, all my experiences, exposures, relationships, learning, and more were part and parcel of what moulded me into being a servant leader.

Indeed I was a servant leader all my life before the term was coined and attempts made to define it. I had no choice! It's just who I was raised to be—a servant leader!

My humble beginnings, my growth and development through the years, and the insights garnered along the way have led me to a deep and ever-deepening understanding and appreciation of the connectivity of all humanity. The kind of spiritual connectivity that draws us together in community to achieve the greatest good for the greatest outcome and impact. It is this understanding that drives my servant leadership.

What prompted me to write this book with focus on servant leadership? You did!

I believe I have a responsibility as a fellow traveler on the journey through life to leave something of value for someone else's onward journey.

I believe that the best lessons in life, particularly leadership lessons, are learnt through the stories we share.

I believe that shared experiences are a powerful tool and are essential in shaping servant leadership.

We each have stories to share, and we should share them. We should be bold enough to be vulnerable and authentic to share the uncomfortable stories, as well as the ones that make us proud.

There are great truths and valuable lessons to be found in all of our stories. Some of the most meaningful lessons are captured and recalled by the tales we tell. They help to shape our values, our norms, and our way of "being."

Vanessa Boris, author at Harvard Business Publishing, states, "Storytelling forges connections among people, and between people and ideas. Stories convey the culture, history, and values that unite people. Without personal life stories to organise our experiences, our own lives would lack coherence and meaning."

In life, there seems never to be enough time to share all the many stories and lessons we need to and should share. I often wish I had the thought, the care, the time, and/or the opportunity to have conversations with many of the people who impacted my life and shaped my path to servant leadership.

Maybe I should have sought out the opportunity to have conversations with Sir Phillip Sherlock and learn more about his life. Perhaps I should have asked my mother more questions about her life. Maybe I could have learnt so much more and become inspired to be of greater service.

I trust that when you have read this book in its entirety, you will remember both the stories and the lessons they convey..

This book ends with a Framework for Action to guide me in performing servant leadership roles in the future.

It consists of a distillation and synthesis of leadership lessons learnt, the core leadership competencies I acquired, and insights I have gleaned from the experiences that contributed to shaping me as a servant leader and making me ready to serve.

I urge you not to head straight for the Framework for Action at the end but to journey with me, page by engaging, lesson-filled page, to the conclusion on the power and transformative capacity of servant leadership.

I write this book to preserve the stories that impacted my life and shaped me as a servant leader and to leave a legacy of lessons that are empowering to you and others.

> A journey is only worth recalling because at some point there were memorable stories tied to the experience. — Anonymous

Introduction

I decided to write this book: Shaping a Servant Leader, at a stage in my life when I have time for serious and in-depth reflection and introspection. The shaping of the book started with two important questions on which I focused while engaging in these processes.

First : What gives purpose and meaning to my life ?

The answer that emerged is that:

My life has purpose and meaning because while I experience personal empowerment I simultaneously help others to empower themselves to improve the quality of their lives.

This brought home to me the philosophical position that this is the essence of what servant leadership is about.

Second: Should I share the processes and outcomes of my being shaped as a Servant Leader with others?

My answer to this question was a resounding YES.

I considered it important to share two important points with individuals preparing to become servant leaders and those who are seasoned leaders who want to add value to their servant leadership endeavours.

The first point is: they can use the significant challenges, and accomplishments along my life's journey that helped to shape my servant leadership, to assess the impact of the different stages of their life's journey on their growth and development as servant leaders.

The second point is : they can use the lessons I learnt, the insights I gleaned and the leadership competencies I acquired to enrich their servant leadership development .

I also considered it important to share my life's journey with young people, especially those who are faced with hardships and challenges each day.

I wish to convey two messages to them.

First, approach hardships and challenges with a creative and positive mindset. Use them as motivational factors to strengthen your self-confidence, self –esteem and your self-reliance capacity.

Second, use hardships and challenges as sources of inspiration and motivation for creating a pathway towards a brighter future and an improved quality of life.

This led me to prepare the first draft of the manuscript ascribing to it the title: Shaping a Servant Leader.

This draft consists of an open and honest narrative of my life *"journey"* - experiences, and people encountered along the way, and how they inspired, influenced and shaped me as a *Servant Leader.*

This draft was further shaped by strategically outlining lessons and insights to facilitate reflection, connection, and mindfulness, of the value and impact of service to others. I paid close attention to the presentation of the narrative to communicate in a clear, simple, cohesive and coherent way by inserting profound *"landmark"* quotes and stories.

This approach was aimed at making the presentation compelling to readers, allowing them to feel as if they are engaged with me live in an inspirational conversation.

The narrative consistently emphasizes three important Guiding Principles that are essential for providing service as a Servant Leader.

Principle 1

Relate : Spend time building relationships with the persons you serve. This creates a portal through which you are allowed to enter and be received into their personal space, thereby enabling you to serve them effectively.

Principle 2

Care : Provide spiritual and psychological support to persons you serve, especially when they have fears and concerns and are experiencing hardships and difficulties.

Principle 3

Share : Use the talents with which God has blessed you to empower those you serve to improve the quality of their lives.

The next stage of shaping the manuscript was twofold , distillation and synthesis. These processes were executed by encapsulating my servant leadership development journey into a Framework for action.

This framework consists of a Leadership Action Toolkit incorporating three major components. These are :

- Leadership lessons Learnt
- Leadership competencies acquired
- Leadership insights gleaned

This toolkit has two major intentions.

First , as a model for me to use as I put into motion transformative initiatives in my continuing journey as a servant leader .

Second, to invite emerging as well as seasoned servant leaders to use this toolkit to enrich the value of their transformative endeavours.

The professional expertise of Glynis Salmon, Bala Press , in the area of manuscript development was invaluable in shaping the manuscript. I combined the differences and complementarity of our perspectives and creative ideas in the continuous refining of the manuscript. During this process particular attention was given to the content, language, tone and flow of the narrative. There was also emphasis on ensuring that the narrative conveys throughout the manuscript, a compelling and inspirational message with laser focus on the important features and value of servant leadership in action.

The final stage of the refinement of the manuscript was copy editing.

The meticulous and professional editorial review by the copy editor of Outskirts Press added value to the quality of the manuscript. This contribution together with my responses prompted by the clarifications and explanations requested and questions raised by the copy editor put the final quality touches on the refinement of the overall manuscript.

The cumulative result of the different stages of shaping the manuscript is its seamless transformation to this book: Shaping a Servant Leader.

The book embodies my primary intention for writing it. This is to inspire readers to move their minds and thoughts to an uplifting level, where they focus simultaneously on empowering themselves and those they serve, to improve the quality of their lives.

1

Raising Up the Servant Leader:
Stories, Lessons, and Impact of Childhood Experiences

> Your childhood dreams and aspirations
> can become your future reality.
> Childhood circumstances shape us profoundly,
> leaving a psychological "residue."
> —Sean Martin

ALL EXPERIENCES IMPACT our attitudes and behaviours as adults, and none more so than those experiences and encounters during the developmental years.

This is especially true for leaders. A critical examination and analysis of any leader would reveal that much of what shaped their leadership character were key childhood moments.

My early childhood experiences and exposures played a pivotal role in shaping me as a servant leader.

I had no other choice, really, than being anything other than a servant leader in any of the many arenas in which, from an early age, I was thrown. I was marked for service and leadership from an early age—in the home, at school, at church, on the playground, and in the community.

My leadership acumen was identified, honed, and developed in lead roles in the "theatre of life," in various scenarios, among my peers. This did not make me superior to anyone else, nor separate from anyone. As the Latin expression so eloquently puts it, I was *primus inter pares* (a leader among equals).

Indeed, all of us as children were each singled out, among ourselves, or by the adults as "special" in one way or another, and for one reason or another. So my "specialness" was not special to only me.

Service as a value and as a virtue was implanted and deeply embedded in me from birth. I was immersed in a bottomless and ever-widening pool of care, selflessness, and focus on the development and empowerment of each other, and of the children in particular, by the village community.

This closely intertwined and interconnected village community of family, neighbours, teachers, and pastors—adults and children—were dynamic, strategic, and impactful in their natural integration of care in each other's lives.

My young and impressionable mind observed, experienced, and took it all in.

In serving others, recognition and rewards were never a consideration by the "villagers." There was a sense in which the villagers shared an innate and compelling wisdom that led to the unified appreciation and respect for the value of *care*, *respect*, and *service*. These attributes formed the bedrock of their individual and communal survival, and the fruition of their hope for the multiplying biblical "abundance" in their lives.

My passion for service is therefore driven by my genuine desire to help others, since from the earliest stages of my life onward, I have been a spectator, participant, and beneficiary to (and of) the nature and character and value of service to others.

As a child, I observed my mother and her relationships with people.

One of the many poignant observations is of my mother facilitating and resolving disputes among community members over breakfast.

The disputing parties who were hell-bent on taking their issues to court would, on their way to said courthouse, stop at our house in the town of Morant Bay for breakfast.

They would have been travelling from the far outlying districts of Trinity Ville, Hillside, and Spring Garden, or other even more far-flung places.

Their appetite for reconciliation may have been dulled by their rancorous conflict, usually about ownership of land, but their appetite for the certain hospitality and refreshing pause they would get in the home and company of my mother united them in singular interest and purpose.

Following all due greetings and salutations, and small talk exchanges with my mother, it would be time for the meal. My mother would always combine the grace with a special prayer for God's divine intervention in the cause for which all the parties were now gathered.

After a few welcomed and rejuvenating mouthfuls, the conversation would lend itself quite naturally into the matter of the pending court case.

As if it were a trial, my mother would preside as judge as the parties in dispute would alternate as prosecutor and defendant in the presentation of their case to my mother.

It didn't take long, however, given my mother's style of adjudication, before the air of social distance and formality was sufficiently relaxed to facilitate civil and reasonable conversation (with some degree of congeniality, I might add) between the disputants.

In most cases, some of these persons who, prior to visiting with my mother, were not on speaking terms with each other, due to the vexation between them, were able to engage in conversations with each other for the first time in ages!

Invariably, after the cups were drained of all the tea (be it coffee or otherwise), the plates cleared of every last bite of the hearty fare, and all "subdued" bodily emissions were expressed amid all the clatter of the serious and lively talk, the parties never made it to the courthouse.

The case was tried right there at the table, with Judge Mama presiding (only to keep order and the arguments on track, not to take sides), and the issues were resolved by the parties themselves, who had by now become "jurors" in their own case.

After such a "trial," there would be much hugging and laughing and shaking of hands, in approval of each other and the agreement and/or decisions arrived at among them.

I would have been taking this all in (unobtrusively of course, since "children should be seen and not heard"), totally unaware of the impact the experience had made on me.

It was not until much later in life that I was made to realize that what I had witnessed with my mother's handling of the issues between conflicting parties is what we now call *alternative dispute resolution* (ADR).

> a govt. official who hears & investigates complaints by private citizens against other officials

It was Donna Parchment Brown, Jamaica's current political ombudsman and former chief executive officer (CEO) of Jamaica's Dispute Resolution Foundation (DRF), who introduced me to this concept and practice of ADR. We had worked together on a project while she served at the DRF, a private voluntary foundation, to establish and encourage the use of ADR techniques throughout Jamaica.

I may not have coordinated and served breakfast as my mother did, but it was from her that I first learnt the rudiments of ADR [the basics], and I later formalized it as an invaluable tool in my leadership toolkit.

I incorporated, to good effect, this ADR approach and process in much of my public service and other leadership roles through the use of social get-togethers, such as parties, lymes (after work relaxation sessions usually with drinks, light refreshments and easy listening music), games, and other recreational activities.

It is truly amazing the degree to which early life experiences can influence future leadership character.

Mark Ocitti, managing director of Serengeti Breweries Limited, in an online article called "Understanding childhood influences on leadership," published by *The Citizen*, made the insightful and powerful point that

> As adults, we more consciously recognise leadership lessons as they appear in classes, meetings, conversations, reading and observation, among others. Some of these lessons stay with us, while others slip away with time.
>
> But one thing remains lasting, and intrinsic in our lives—the ingrained leadership traits that we exhibit unconsciously, occasioned by our childhood experiences—which has instilled lessons that shape our ability as a leader, to have a stronger, more positive leadership impact.

Amy Wolfgang, executive and leadership coach, endorses Mark Ocitti's point in her online article on "How my childhood experiences influenced my leadership style." She writes, "Our unconscious mind is powerful. We need to be aware of how our subconscious childhood mind plays out in our lives…and impact our adult world."

My mother was a truly exceptional woman. Her care for others knew no bounds. She helped her friends who could not read or write to feel comfortable and utilize, each in their own way, creative ways to respond to and overcome this challenge.

She operated from a "strengths-based" position and affirmed the gifts of people, even as she encouraged and inspired others to unearth or cultivate new skills and talents.

She empowered and enabled people to "rise" and "shine" and give full expression to their capacity to live purpose and make a positive difference in their own and others' lives.

No one would be allowed to "hide their light under a bushel" under her watch. Even if it was to participate in church and community functions by speaking, singing, dancing, drama, or other types of performance, everyone had to find their "light" and let it shine.

Needless to say, I was a regular *peenie-wallie* (Jamaican name for firefly) at all these social events.

There was a very good friend of my mother's, whose husband migrated to England with the promise that once he was settled there, he would send for her to join him. He would send her a letter each month, which she would ask me to read to her.

I had to serve both as the reader and the language interpreter all at once. I read the letter to her in the native Jamaican language or dialect—*patois* pronounced "pat-wah"—that she could understand. She would then dictate a reply to the letter in her own *patois* language and styling, which I would translate into standard English.

As if that were not enough, she then would ask me to read back to her what I had written, as she had dictated, to ensure that all she wanted to say to her husband was captured exactly as she said it and in exactly the way she said it. To complete the process, I then had to read it back to her in the exact language she had used.

I may have found the process to be often quite tedious and sometimes confusing, but I was always aware of the privileged position in which I was placed and the high regard in which my service was held (with or without a reward).

Most importantly, I learnt two valuable lessons from this interaction, which I have found to be invaluable, as I engaged with people from diverse socioeconomic and educational backgrounds.

Servant Leadership Lessons

Lesson 1: Trust is of fundamental importance in your relationship with the people you serve.

Trusting is a process of establishing and nurturing lasting bonds of hearts, minds, and souls with the persons you serve.

Treasure that trust and strive continuously to keep that bond intact.

There will be persons, young or old, who may invite you into their confidence and invest their trust in your ability to share in, and not betray, sometimes very private aspects of their life. Be confidential and honour their trust.

Lesson 2: Be sensitive to and respectful of people's sociocultural realities.

You should invest time in knowing, understanding, and appreciating, without judgement or bias, the varying cultures of people and the environment in which you operate.

These two lessons—(1) trust and (2) respecting the sociocultural realities of persons you serve—were well-learnt in my childhood years, through the dynamics of my letter reading and writing assignments, which served me well.

In every organization in which I have served, these lessons were pivotal [of crucial importance] in performing my servant leadership role with both internal and external stakeholders,

I believe very strongly that effective communication can only take place when there is mutuality in interest, understanding, and expected outcomes. Mutuality [sharing of a feeling] is not automatic; it must be facilitated.

I had to meet my mother's friend where she was, academically, and enable her to meet her goal. Together we were quite satisfied with the outcome, and I was rewarded by the impact on my servant leadership character.

On a Sunday, once per month, I had to accompany my mother to visit the sick at the hospital, where she offered them hope and comfort through prayers and kind conversation.

I didn't know then that my mother was in fact modeling what would become a fundamental part of my character, applied in leadership and in all other areas of my life.

Servant Leadership Lesson

Spiritual and psychological support is very important in our relationships with the people we serve, especially when they are going through difficult situations/periods in their life.

Increasingly, studies show the value of nurturing and sustaining the "mind-soul connection" for the wellness and well-being of people.

While there were undoubtedly other influences and influencers, it was my mother who had the greatest influence and impact in shaping my character and servant leadership characteristics.

One of the most fundamental characteristics of being a human being and being a servant leader is *care*—prioritizing the needs of others over narrow self-interest and vain ambitions.

My mother took me several steps further along in understanding and appreciating the value and impact of care, and adopting and practicing a holistic approach—integrating mind, body, and soul—in the care of others.

Through observing her self-sacrificial mission of care to the sick, the process of emulating her as a role model—to inform my own character as a servant leader—was set in motion.

The relationship between the behaviours of the role models—in particular, our parents—and our core beliefs, principles, and practices as an adult and as a leader cannot be overlooked or discounted.

With every person, experience, encounter, or incident that we come across in our daily lives, particularly in our childhood, learning opportunities and lessons take place.

My mother, by taking me with her on her monthly Sunday visits to the hospital, must have known the significance and importance of childhood role models and was therefore deliberate in her intent to integrate role modeling in my growth and development.

The observation of what to do and how to behave as a human being, through the positive effect of my mother's holistic care of others, was particularly profound in the development of my servant leadership character.

Indeed, it was my mother, more than anyone else, who inspired and enabled my choice and my growth as a servant leader.

When I was growing up, another feature of my home and family environment was that children—whose parents, for one reason or another, left them at our house ostensibly for a short visit—would sometimes get "drafted" into and grafted on to our family tree as our "brothers and sisters."

These new members of our family would have to go through a process of socialization that sought to bring them into alignment with my mother's unequivocal values, principles, and expectations. They had to quickly adjust and get in shape and fall in line with the rest of the family.

My mother would relentlessly drill into us, certain (in her book) absolute and non-negotiable "laws of life." One of them was the importance of education. She would firmly impress upon us (brooking no opposition in attitude or behaviour) to "take education seriously, attend school regularly, and do well!"

I will never forget those words. Nor will I ever cease to be amazed by my mother's way of being. Her care for others and her deep desire to serve as an empowering and transforming agent in people's lives, particularly the children, impacted me greatly.

It is even more remarkable to me when I realize, upon reflection, that her willingness and readiness to embrace, house, and raise other people's children as her own belied her already burdened [disguised] economic resources.

Unlike the "old lady who lived in a shoe, and had so many children, she didn't know what to do," my mother did not acknowledge lack or limitations. She operated from what I now know to be a "growth mindset" and filtered life only through possibilities and a vision for a bright future.

She afforded all of us children in the home, whether we were her biological children or not, equal benefits and opportunities, and she reinforced in all of us the values and principles that would enable us to "reach far in life."

I believe that all of our childhood experiences come into play in shaping our adult life and the character of our leadership. Some aspects may become fixed at a young age, while others are developed later.

I believe that the experiences of our childhood contribute immensely to equipping us with the tools to live positively and purposefully, to lead and serve effectively, to affect individual and community change, and to impress and impact generations.

When later in life my wife, Esther, and I decided that in addition to parenting our own child, we would parent other children, I knew that the seeds of parenting, guidance, and counselling were planted in me, from childhood, by my mother. For it was my mother who first introduced me to this concept and practice of *expansive parenting*, and whose purpose and mission I modeled.

Esther and I have "raised" (been parents for) over thirty children. As my mother had indelibly imprinted in my consciousness, "take education seriously," we undertook the total responsibility of putting all of our children through elementary school, high school, and some through colleges and universities, in addition to seeing to their holistic growth and development

My greatest satisfaction is to see them, as adults, putting into practice the positive values and attitudes that we endeavoured to pass on to them.

I have wryly noted, with a mix of bemusement and pride, that those of our children who gave us the most trouble while growing up have become responsible and exemplary parents.

I am actually having fun while reflecting upon, and sharing with you, these observations about my children's experiences as adults and as parents.

One of the girls complained recently that her daughter was talking back to her and disagreeing with everything she said. I burst out into hearty laughter, which prompted the somewhat belligerent response, "What was so funny?" To which I replied, "She is behaving just like you did when you were growing up!"

I doubt she was amused by the reminder, but I certainly was.

While driving with one of the boys one evening, I said to him, "I pray that your son will give you even fifty percent of the trouble you gave me while you were growing up."

In response, his immediate and spontaneous outburst was an emphatic "No! No! No! Don't wish that on me!"

I chuckled at the irony.

Through the years, Esther and I, as my mother did years ago, realized that the love we had for our children had to be shared equitably and understood clearly. There could be no shade of difference or shadow of doubt.

This was brought home forcibly to us one day when we overheard three of the now adult children arguing among themselves about who was "first son," "first daughter," and "first child."

The three in question are constantly teasing and poking fun at each other. Their playfulness, however, can sometimes mask the seriousness of their banter.

This "first this or that" argument had nothing to do with chronological age, but as you may have guessed, it had to do with hierarchy of importance and affection.

They are never afraid of, nor do they shy away from ranking their status and positioning in our lives as parents. To them an acknowledgment of being "first" cemented the fact that they were the preferred *el numero uno/#1!*—and held pride of place in our affections and interest in them.

In addition to which, and perhaps more importantly to them, being first entitled them to more of everything, especially Esther's famed pea soup, prized mangoes…and, of course, more individual attention.

I grew up in a "big yard" (in later years called a "tenement yard"), in my Jamaican reality. Later in life I found out that in the "big yard" I was experiencing the practical application of the African Proverb "It takes a village to raise a child."

Two complementary versions of concepts and practices related to this proverb were applicable to my experiences in the "big yard."

First , the version in an excerpt from the Article ," It takes a Village to raise a Child" by Van der Rheede, Christo , 2010:

"This profound wisdom, commitment, compassion, considerateness and caring of each other's children prevailed over centuries in many African villages. Through unsophisticated and simple traditions and teachings, generation upon generation was raised with values, skills, knowledge and wisdom to survive and prosper, but more importantly to reap from and to live in harmony with nature."

Second the version in an excerpt from the Article," Community Preparedness: It takes a Village " by Robert James and Kim Farley published in the American Journal of Public Health, September 10, 2019 :

"The phrase embodies the concept of a whole community interacting for the well-being, safety, and health of all, particularly vulnerable populations such as children."

There were two houses in my yard. We lived in the main house, in which two of the rooms were rented out. One of these rooms was occupied by a talented artist, Vincent Cameron, who served in World War II and came home from England with a bachelor of arts (BA) degree.

A college or university degree in those days was a huge accomplishment, as it still is, but even more so then. It gave the holder almost demi-God status in a community peopled with many who could not read or write.

Mr. Cameron tried to teach me art and art appreciation. He also tried to raise my consciousness and awareness of important global events. I remember that he always ended our conversations by saying to me, "You are going to be a great man."

I did not quite fathom at the time what he meant, but he spoke those words so feelingly and with such confidence that it sounded good to me and made me feel good about myself too! I often wondered, "What did he see in me?"

I later realized that he was putting the Pygmalion effect into action to get me to focus on aspiring toward and maintaining a high standard of performance.

a psychological phenomenon in which high expectations lead to improved performance

To quote Wikipedia, "The Pygmalion effect, or Rosenthal effect, is a psychological phenomenon wherein high expectations lead to improved performance in a given area.

"The effect is named after the Greek myth of Pygmalion, a sculptor who fell in love with a statue he had carved, or alternately, after the psychologist Robert Rosenthal, who held that high expectations lead to better performance and low expectations lead to worse."

So Mr. Cameron, by speaking my "greatness" into being, held out to me an extraordinarily high expectation that he hoped I would work toward achieving. Now that was motivation!

It is not for me to assess my so-called greatness, but I sure worked hard at achieving and exceeding, in some instances, the high expectations others had set for me, as well as those I had set for myself.

I am quite taken by Mark Ocitti, whom I quoted earlier in this chapter. His insights on "Understanding Childhood Influences in Leadership" are quite profound.

To underscore the far-reaching impact of childhood experiences on adulthood and leadership, Ocitti is worth quoting again:

"While it's a fact that from childhood onward our brains develop as we grow older, our early interpretations of events and people form beliefs that we carry into adulthood. It is in childhood that we start to create a self-identity and shape our leadership traits."

Now back to the big yard in which I grew up...

Two of my cousins, far older than I, lived in two rooms of the other four-room house in the yard. The two remaining rooms were occupied by other tenants. One of my cousins taught me to read the time on the clock, and the other taught me how to measure a piece of lumber, i.e., length, width, and thickness.

From them I learnt basic mathematical skills. My mother, on the other hand, was the reading specialist and helped me greatly to develop reading skills.

I recall that it might have been about two weeks after I had been in basic school that my mother, much to her dismay, discovered that I could not recognize the letters of the alphabet. Well, she took both me and my book "up in hand," and there ended my attendance at basic school, and hence came my enrollment in Mama Home School. .

Mama began my home school experience by placing me in a "classroom" beside the wash pan. As she steadily washed clothes, I dutifully paid attention to her lessons.

In between the squish-squish-squishing of her washing, she taught me the sound of each letter of the alphabet and how to combine these sounds to make words. This was called the *phonetic method* or *phonometic awareness*, as I later learnt as a student at Mico College, now Mico University College.

My older brother would make time to discuss various topics with me, including sports, music, current affairs, and major social and cultural events in our parish, and in other parishes across Jamaica. He was a cricket enthusiast and umpire, as well as an expert on musical selections played on sound systems—the juke box and the radio.

The net result of the combined efforts of my family's intervention in my educational development was that by the time I entered the formal school system, at six years old, I was already far in advance of my class.

I was enrolled and placed in what was then called A class. Such a class was intended for beginners, foundational learning students. I was, however, an already well-rounded and well-grounded student. I was a fluent reader, reading the Bible, the newspaper (the *Gleaner*), and other literature. I also knew the fundamentals of arithmetic and could easily grasp, apply, and master basic mathematical principles.

My interest in sports was also well developed, and I was quite the fledgling all-around sportsman. In addition, I had developed an ear for music and was also quite good at it.

Consequently, after about two weeks of being enrolled in A class, I was placed in first class.

When I completed first class, I was promoted to third class. I was then moved to fourth class and further promoted to sixth class.

For the younger readers of this book, it is important to pause at this juncture and place the elementary school in Jamaica in a historical context.

The elementary school was part of our colonial heritage. Elementary schooling consisted of eight stages: A class, B class, first class, second class, third class, fourth class, fifth class, and sixth class.

Comparing it with our preset system, A class through fourth class is equivalent to grades one through six in our primary schools; fifth class and sixth class are equivalent to grades seven and nine at the junior high and high schools.

Elementary level schooling was very important for the mass of the population, since only the children of "privileged persons," such as rich landowners, bank managers, Anglican Church ministers, medical doctors, members of the judiciary, school principals, rich merchants, and shopkeepers, had the option of going to private schools (especially those with boarding facilities, such as Munro, Hampton, St. Andrew High, and Jamaica College).

In that era, my parish, St. Thomas, had no high schools, and my family was not a member of the privileged group.

Elementary school students could sit for three local examinations: First Jamaica Local, Second Jamaica Local, and Third Jamaica Local Examination.

Students would normally sit for the First Jamaica Local Examination at the end of the fifth or sixth class, and subsequently, sit for the Second and Third Jamaica Local exams.

After passing the first exam, you can become a monitor to assist a class teacher with minor duties. After passing the second exam, you can get a supernumerary position, which is somewhat like a teaching assistant position. After passing the third test, you can be hired for a paid teaching position as a probationer.

The Third Jamaica Local Examination Certificate satisfied the matriculation requirements for entering teacher education institutions, such as The Mico, Shortwood, St. Joseph, and Bethlehem, or Jamaica School of Agriculture, the School of Nursing at the Kingston Pubic Hospital (KPH), or the University Hospital of the West indies (UHWI).

Your counterparts at high schools would do UK-based examinations, such as Junior Cambridge and Senior Cambridge.

Senior Cambridge was replaced by the General Certificate Examination (GCE) and later by the Caribbean Secondary Examination Certificate (CSEC), set by the Caribbean Examination Council (CXC).

While attending elementary school, I did not envisage that I would later in life become the chairman of the Overseas Examinations Commission (OEC), which is the body responsible for administering local and overseas examinations in Jamaica, and technical adviser in measurement and evaluation for CXC.

As I reflect on my early childhood, I wish all those who impacted my life so profoundly when I was a child were still alive to witness and enjoy my accomplishments in later years.

I would have so loved for them to have known how much of my success is credited to them. I am happy that my late mother and my late older brother were at my graduation from Mico College and the University of the West Indies (UWI).

I close this chapter with thoughts on the value and importance of influencers in the early childhood development of servant leaders.

Though much of what happens in our childhood is out of our control, how we choose to experience and interpret those events is very much in our control.

We cannot choose our ethnicity, nationality, community, or family that we are born into. We cannot choose the culture and events around us that greatly impact our identity, opportunities, and worldview.

We always have the ability, however, to choose our response, our interpretations, and our subsequent actions.

As children, this is often learnt from our parents and others, such as spiritual leaders, teachers, and friends, who have the ability to influence us.

We emulate those we respect and love. If we see them seeking to rise above the pressures and norms, to choose hope over despair, and to not be defined by external factors, how much greater is our potential to become like them.

In early childhood you may lay the foundation of poverty or riches, industry or idleness, good or evil, by the habits to which you train your children; teach them right habits then, and their future life is safe. —Lydia Sigourney

2

Growing Up the Servant Leader:
Stories, Lessons, and Impact of Boyhood Experiences

> Certain situations inherently bring out leadership
> skills and qualities.
> Sometimes these characteristics are raw and un-nurtured
> and other times they are developed and applied in great
> deliberation.
> —Kirstin Davidson

ALL OF LIFE'S experiences, at whatever age, stage, or circumstance, affect and impact our lives and shape our character. Every day we live, there are learning opportunities and lessons in all of our experiences and encounters.

Regrettably, so many people are unaware of, or gloss over, their life stories without recognizing the valuable life and leadership lessons they contain.

Morgan W. McCall Jr., an academic, posits that "the primary source of learning to lead, to the extent that leadership can be learnt, is experience."

This is not to say that training is unimportant to shaping a leader, but it pales in significance to experiential learning.

There is no doubt in my mind that a combination of learning from experience, reflecting on those experiences, and connecting with the lessons is key to shaping a leader.

Certainly much of the experiences, observations, reflections, and lessons learnt from my early boyhood years have greatly influenced my thinking, my way of being, and the character of my servant leadership.

Throughout my boyhood, beyond the formal lessons learnt in school, I have learnt so many other valuable and vital lessons that have served as important stepping-stones in my leadership journey.

The stories of my life are very poignant. They have enabled me to cultivate and sharpen my self-awareness (a key tool in the servant leader's toolkit).

This self-awareness has enabled me to demonstrate my strengths and recognize my weaknesses, and it has strengthened my capacity to effectively lead and influence others.

The following stories from my life, particularly those culled from my boyhood experiences, will illustrate some of the many leadership lessons I have learnt during this period of my life.

Servant Leadership Lesson

Use the talents with which God has blessed you to survive, cope, and break down social barriers and restrictive systems, as well as opportunities to strengthen your self-confidence and self-worth.

My boyhood was spent in Morant Bay, St. Thomas, Jamaica. In my hometown, Morant Bay, clear lines were drawn between the rich and the poor. Two examples of places where there was evidence of this divide were the Anglican Church and the Morant Bay Tennis Club.

On our days of worship at the Anglican Church, the first three pews/rows of benches (made of fine cedar wood) were reserved for the elite of the town. Wealth and/or social status defined members of this elite group, which included the Custos of the parish, the manager of Barclays Bank D. C.O.(Dominion Colonial and Overseas), and large estate and landowners and their families.

Less affluent persons sat in descending order from the benches behind the first three reserved pews at the front to the back of the church, each according to their economic and social status.

I learnt how to deal with this system of seating by becoming a member of the choir, which sat right up front, near the pulpit and the pipe organ.

This social divide also was evident at the Morant Bay Tennis Club. Membership in this club was reserved exclusively for the town's elite, defined by their wealth and social status.

I became a ball boy at the Morant Bay Tennis Club. In this position, I began the process of learning how to play the game of lawn tennis with its peculiar point-score system of 15, 30, 40—with the possibility of fault or double fault—to eventual game!

My colleagues who are more versed in the subject of history inform me that these social stratifications, and the practices thereof, were remnants from the vestry and plantocracy systems, which we inherited and carried on from our British colonial past.

To reinforce the point, they reminded me that the Anglican Church was in close proximity to the courthouse. Both of these church and state symbols of governance figured prominently in one of Jamaica's most catalytic sociohistorical events: the Morant Bay Rebellion led by national hero Paul Bogle.

Later in life, on one of my visits to my hometown after I had completed my studies at The Mico and UWI, I was invited to sit in the highly prized and coveted front seat at the Anglican Church.

I guess I had arrived and could be recognized as being "somebody."

These experiences give credence to the statement that "education is an agent of upward social mobility."

Servant Leadership Lesson

Collaboration and teamwork benefit everyone.

The economic challenges that had beset my family when I was growing up in my dynamic single-parent, biological-and-acquired-siblings, family blend meant that we could not afford to buy fish.

Fish then, and now, is ranked high on the leader board of costs for "fish-kind" (a *Jamaicanism* to describe any flesh, found on land or sea, that would be prepared as the main course in a meal).

clever, original or inventive

I had long ago observed my mother's ingenuity and resourcefulness. She acknowledged challenges as a bridge to opportunities. She chose to be solution-driven, rather than anxiety-ridden.

Modeling my mother's innovative "can do," results-oriented, and goal–focused approach to life and living, I determined that if we could not afford to buy fish, there were other ways we could "net" the precious "catch" for our cook pot.

I therefore set out to become a friend of the fishermen—not with a beggarly intent but to position myself as a valuable help to them.

When the fishermen drew *seine*—which according to Wikipedia and what I know to be so from my experience is a "method of fishing that employs the use of a fishing net, or seine, that hangs vertically in the water with its bottom edge held down by weights, and its top edge buoyed by floats"—I would voluntarily help them to pull in the net. As a reward, I would get some herring, cutlass fish, jack, kingfish, and sprats.

After the boat collected the nets from deep sea fishing, I was also, again voluntarily, a part of the crew that helped to pull in the boat, which was then placed on rollers made out of the wood from coconut trees. My reward was getting fish such as parrot, butterfish, and snapper.

Needless to say, with this approach my family was never wanting for fish on the menu. In addition, my boyhood experiences were enriched by exciting adventures at sea, learning new skills, and expanding my knowledge of the sea, seasons, weather, fish, fishing, and so much more.

Most importantly, I developed and established close relationships with the fishermen, which gave me access to a font of invaluable life lessons.

The fact that I was also, though still a boy, making a meaningful contribution to my family's resources, and the variation of the menu, filled me with both pride and joy.

I felt like quite the "little man," and my family and the community respected and responded to me as such (not that it made me exempt from, or immune to, reprimand should I dare be out of order or attempt to get out of hand).

Servant Leadership Lesson

The difficulties that we experience in life can motivate us to find creative solutions.

In the case of the seine fish, my family's preferred choice of accompaniment was bread. There was nothing nicer to us than bread with fish. We thoroughly enjoyed such a hearty and delicious meal. The problem was finding enough money to buy the bread.

The solution? Purchase "reduce bread"!

Once per week, the bakery would collect from different shops the bread that was supplied to them but not sold. This unsold bread would be taken back to the bakery. The bread, dubbed "stale bread," was then sold by the bakery, at a reduced price; hence the term "reduce bread."

This reduce bread that prior to its staleness would have cost, for instance, one shilling per loaf would now, in its reduced state, cost three pence—a quarter of the price!

We would buy this stale bread, scrape off any *junjo* (fungus) that might be present, and then put it on the hot coals from the wood fire to toast. Believe me when I tell you, no "fresh" bread has ever tasted better! And with the fish, it was a feast fit for a king! It was simply delicious.

Servant Leadership Lesson

True friendship is mutually beneficial.

I became friends with a gentleman who would travel all the way from Manchester every Friday to sell yams at the Morant Bay Market.

I would be there as soon as the truck came in. I would then help him unload the yams and pack them in heaps—yam display mounds—ready for sale!

He would always bring two special pieces of yam for me.

My mother also sold at the market. The main items she had for sale were black pepper and curry powder. Of course, I was my mother's handy helper, assisting her with everything but especially with the selling.

The market was a rich source of wisdom and learning that yielded up a bounty of wisdom, knowledge, skills, insight, and inspiration to me. It taught me so much, and I learnt so much more from the experience.

I learnt how to get the best price for the goods we sold and how to sell more by "marrying" one item with another, i.e., putting together a combination of items that were in demand and in scarce supply, with other slow-moving items.

I sometimes created attractive and appealing "bundle deals" by combining seasonal items, such as plantains and breadfruit, with other complementary items.

I also learnt to make quick mathematical calculations in my head and, just as quickly, make the correct change in pounds, shillings, and pence. These were important applied skills for developing my mathematical competencies.

My mother was a skillful dressmaker and made and sold underpants to cane cutters. Her original and special design for the very popular underpants she made was, I prefer to think, the precursor to a later design in equally popular demand that we now call "boxer shorts."

My mother like all other vendors had to sell outside the gate of the Serge Island sugar factory. In those days, we could not venture past the gate into "the white people them place."

Years later, when I was corporate vice president at the head office of the ICD Group of companies and a director of Serge island Dairies, I was saluted by the security guard as I drove in for board meetings—through the same gates my mother and I were not fit to put our foot through all those many years ago. What a difference in attitude with the passage of time!

Back to the underpants...

My mother would "trust" the buyers these items, i.e., give them to the buyer on credit and collect payment weeks later.

I would then be pressed into service by my mother as a bill collector. In that role, I had to take the bus from Morant Bay to places like Trinity Ville to collect payment for these underpants.

I had to develop the art of bill collecting. I learnt to start the collecting rounds with those who owed the most and for more than two months. I would walk to their houses just when they were having Sunday dinner after church. Over time, I became quite adept at bill collection and was hugely successful.

Later, when I worked in the corporate world, I learnt that this was accounts receivable to which we applied practices such as "aging" and the 80/20 rule, i.e., focusing on collecting from the 20 percent of customers who tended to owe 80 percent of the total amount owed to you.

Marilyn Price-Mitchell, PhD, founder of Roots of Action, made the profound i observation that "the roots of leadership are being nurtured...through a young person's relationships and life experiences."

3

Schooling the Servant Leader:
Stories, Lessons, and Impact of Elementary Schooling

IT'S ELEMENTARY!

Schooling at all levels—basic school, elementary school, high school, college, and university—plays a pivotal role in shaping who we are as adults and leaders.

It is an amazing part of life's journey and experiences and provides a rich cache of so many important lessons, inside and outside the classroom.

The compelling influence of school experiences, particularly at the elementary level, in impacting and shaping leadership development is unquestionable and inescapable.

Some unforgettable moments in school will live with us for the rest of our lives. Some incidences, too, that we thought would happen only in school, we discover in later years also happen in our daily lives as adults and also in the workforce.

Since childhood we have responded to the influences of individuals who were role models, be they parents, siblings, extended family, teachers, coaches, friends, and other members of our society with whom we come in contact.

Exposure to these role models may have been through the home, school, church, sports, entertainment, or myriad other places and social activity.

There is no one, and certainly no *one* leader, who upon review and examination of their life's journey would not include the impact of their schooling on shaping their character and their leadership characteristics.

I know that some of the most impactful sets of influencing experiences that helped to shape me as a servant leader were during the period of my elementary schooling.

During my elementary school days I did not own a book. That is to say, I did not own, for me, a book for recreational reading or a textbook. In those days the standard textbook in my elementary school was the *West Indian Reader*. Each volume, from first class to sixth class, had wonderful stories with great morals for life.

There were many positive features about not owning a book, however.

I would memorize each book I borrowed from the library from cover to cover, including pauses for commas, semicolons, colons, and full stops.

I remember my teacher being dumbstruck when I recited, verbatim, an entire chapter from a history book on the major earthquake at Port Royal in 1692.

Truth is, I seemed to have developed from an early age a photographic memory, or perhaps I was born with the "gift." In later years, the skill of visualization and use of mental images was also added.

These skills were to be of tremendous help and value to me, as well as to the several organizations where I served in key leadership roles, including board chairman or director, and as a "ritualist" in my Freemason lodge.

Of course, it was also a skill I utilized to great effect in my schoolwork and in extracurricular activities, such as drama, which made learning scripts a cinch! [easy task]

The library was a rich repository and vital source for information and knowledge, beyond what was conveyed to me in the classroom. As such, I grew up having a great respect for the parish library.

With its seemingly limitless supply of books and access to information, the library was also the "pass" and the path to access other critical assets, chief of which was the wonderful bevy of bright and beautiful young ladies, whom I would meet and admire in muted interest, between the covers of a book.

The other exciting, but not quite as attractive, appeal of the library was that my friend David Telfer and I would research data that we would pass on to the men at the barbershop in our hometown (known by most people at the time as Stervel Foster's Barbershop).

The men who would gather at the barbershop were always engaged in betting on a variety of subjects, including sports, world affairs, music, and history.

David and I would supply our "client" with the data on a particular subject that we had gleaned from the library. Our client would in turn use that information to his advantage on a bet.

Such a client, if he was skillful in the use of the data we provided, would win the bet not only handsomely but also in the much sought-after bragging rights to being a brain.

Of course, David and I would get a cut as payment from the client's winnings. David always got the larger share of the money because he would be the "lead researcher" on facts about the ever-popular game of cricket.

This was a sport in which most men of that era had not just a passionate interest but also were vicarious "heroes" of the game, each ascribing to themselves the prowess of the real players, past or present, that they most admired.

It was from those early elementary school days that David's and my thriving entrepreneurial pursuits with the men at Stervel Foster's Barbershop began its development path.

It was then, too, that I began to form a notion about one of the key fundamentals of marketing: focus on those things for which most customers have the greatest passionate need.

Interestingly, the library that was for me, in my younger years, the gateway to knowledge and girls (not always in that order of importance) was to become later in life one of my institutional charges, as chairman of the National Council for Libraries, Archives, and Information Systems.

My class teacher at elementary school was Mr. Conex Jarrett (the father of Hon. Earl Jarrett, OJ, chief executive officer of the Jamaica National Group) and a MICO man. He offered me free private lessons when I was preparing for the First Jamaica Local Examination.

There was no discussion about payment, given my economic circumstance and the likely inability to pay for the lessons, just a silent understanding.

His generosity of spirit was matched only by his strength of character, which led him to seek me out for regular discussions to affirm my scholastic capacity and his faith in my ability to be an exhibitioner when I sat for the Jamaica local examinations.

In the sessions with him, each afternoon after regular classes, his friend Ashbel, who was a banana checker, would invariably be present and join in the discussions.

I admired this banana checker, who was renowned for his amazing ability to just look at a bunch of bananas, quickly assess, and in no time—almost immediately—declare that the banana in question was a "seven-hand, eight-hand," or other numbered bunch! He was always correct.

I thought this man was a genius! He was a real marvel. In addition, his penmanship was impeccable. He wrote so beautifully, and to cap it all, he earned very good pay.

So when both he and Teacher Jarrett would extoll my academic virtues and envision for me success in the Jamaica local examinations, I could not comprehend what it all meant. But of one thing I was certain and very clear about: I wanted to be a banana checker!

Surely, this was not the professional destiny that Teacher Jarrett had in mind for me, with all this talk about abilities in the presence of the esteemed banana checker, upon whom I could model my career aspirations.

So altogether, I resolved to become a banana checker! Alas this was not to be…

When I did in fact sit for the First Jamaica Local Examination, I was successful not only in passing the exam but also in ranking second on the island, with distinction in arithmetic. I received, along with widespread applause and acclaim in my community, the grand prize of fifteen shillings! I was an exhibitioner.

My mother used this princely sum to buy me cream-colored serge pants, which in those days were at the height of sartorial dapperness and appeal to the young ladies. I was ecstatic, more so by my improved social status with the ladies than by the scholarship.

An intriguing part of this story is how my elementary school headmaster, D.R.B. Grant, a MICO man (who has been credited with being the father of early childhood education in Jamaica), shared with me the information about the examination results.

When the results were published, D.R.B. sent for me to come to his office. He and his wife, Gene, also a teacher at the school, showed me my name in a document.

My initial thought was that perhaps his "summons" had to do with the Parish Choir Competition, which would be held in about two weeks' time, and in which I would be participating as the lead singer in the boys' choir.

This was an event that our teacher, Mr. Jarrett, had spent weeks preparing us for, with the motivation that if we won at the parish level, we would get a chance to perform at the prestigious Ward Theatre in Kingston.

The upcoming Parish Choir Competition was what was uppermost in my mind when I showed up in the headmaster's office in response to his call.

He showed me a document with my name on it. I was quite clueless about why, other than the upcoming competition, my name was on an official-looking document. Recognizing the abject absence of any understanding or appreciation on my part of the meaning and significance of the document at hand, the headmaster proceeded to, and was at pains to, explain it all to me.

He perhaps gave his many explanations to me several times, even going over it all, again and again, from the beginning. So much for being a "bright boy." I was still lost.

The headmaster's wife, Gene; Teacher Jarrett; and Teacher Joyce Brown (who later married Teacher Jarrett) were all present in unified and animated support of whatever information it was that the headmaster was trying to convey to me.

With a great deal of calm and even greater effort, such as would be taken with one who was considered a dullard, D.R.B. once again explained to me, very slowly and carefully, that the document with my name in it was called the *Gazette*. This was the first time I was exposed to this important national document.

One of the items that was published in the *Gazette*, D.R.B. explained, was examination results. He further explained that my name was in a special section of the *Gazette* because I had earned the distinction of passing my exam and placing second on the entire island, with "distinction in arithmetic."

I may not have fully grasped the value and significance of this accomplishment, but I felt proud nonetheless that I had put my parish, St. Thomas, on the map, so to speak!

This event became the introduction to a lifetime relationship between Headmaster Grant and me. He has been my mentor since then, consistently throughout the years, in all stages of my academic and professional development.

I modeled my own mentor relationship with the several persons whom I had the great privilege of mentoring on the relationship I shared with D.R.B. Grant.

Each year I sponsor at least two bright and financially challenged students through college and university. I engage them in conversations focused on enabling them to build a positive image of themselves. I encourage them to identify and claim their value and worth.

They are empowered to give full expression to the vast capabilities that God has so richly blessed them with and that persons have vested their interest and resources in unearthing and developing.

The influence of role models, such as Headmaster D.R.B. Grant, Teacher Jarrett, Mr. "Banana Checker," and many others, on my elementary school journey has led me to foster and maintain a genuine, meaningful, and mutually enriching relationship with the students whom I sponsor.

These role models also led me to embrace the value and importance of elevating guidance and counselling over and beyond financial assistance.

The guiding Servant Leadership Philosophy that I formulated from this experience is as follows:

Servant Leadership Philosophy

When you are nurturing and assisting others, focus on developing a relationship with them that conveys that you genuinely care about them as individuals. This is more important than your financial support if you are going to make a positive difference in their lives.

I am grateful to all who have taught me by lived example that in order to honour my intention to make a positive and transformative difference in the lives of others, it is vital to develop and establish a meaningful, nurturing relationship, motivated by genuine care for the welfare and well-being of others.

Such a relationship will be far more beneficial and far-reaching than all the money I could ever contribute.

As my mother did with all her children, I impressed upon my mentees the value of education and the importance of getting and maintaining high grades.

I sought also, as Teacher Jarrett did with me, to enlighten and empower my mentees with the fact that no barriers or limitations, socioeconomic or otherwise, in their lives can disqualify their claim to success.

What society may seek to impose upon them as disqualifiers—their address, upbringing, orientation, associations—can in fact, if they are prepared to take "the road less travelled," be the ultimate qualifier to claiming and expressing their intrinsic greatness and realizing great accomplishments for the good of themselves and others.

I strongly believe that we all have the ability to rise above our circumstances. Whatever comes our way, we have the capacity to develop characteristics that are absolutely crucial to successful adulthood and leadership.

I remain mindful, and use it as a source of inspiration to others, that I grew up in a 'big yard', but there were no boundaries to the estate of my ambitions and my capacity to achieve excellence.

The cumulative impact of our experiences and the lessons learnt from schooling, in both formal and informal educational settings (for all of life's experiences are an education), contribute to shaping us to be effective servant leaders.

4

Developing the Servant Leader:
Stories, Lessons, and Impact of the High School Years

> Leadership is not a job title.
> It's a character trait that schools seek to cultivate in each student and extend to all stakeholders to develop, support, and guide the leadership qualities of students.
> —Dr. Suzanne Bean

FROM VERY EARLY in life, leadership begins to take root and take shape. As Dr. Suzanne Bean, director of the Roger F. Wicker Center for Creative Learning, says

> Leadership permeates all dimensions of life, across all disciplines, ages, cultures, and socioeconomic levels of society ...and involves thinking creatively and critically, making difficult decisions, communicating ideas clearly, and being an ethical person...It includes demonstrating these skills in everyday personal and school environments.

The development of young leaders is an integral part of schooling. In purposeful and intentional ways, the school environment is engineered toward creating young leaders. Students at any age can learn valuable leadership skills that can help them as they grow.

I ended up at a technical high school (Dinthill Technical High School) as winner of the St. Thomas Parish Scholarship.

Having passed the First Jamaica Local Examination and placed second on the island, I boldly decided, in spite of opposition and against all odds, to skip the Second Jamaica Local Examination and move forward to the Third Jamaica Local Examination.

This was my first attempt at entering uncharted waters, independent of support from my teachers, most of whom did not agree with my decision.

As such, in preparation for the examination, I now had to fend for myself as it were, and undertake the arduous and dubious task of tutoring myself for most of the subjects, including arithmetic.

While I was preparing for the Third Jamaica Local Examination, on the advice of my headmaster and mentor, D.R.B. Grant, and my teacher, Mr. Jarrett, I also prepared and sat for the parish scholarship examination.

In those days each parish had two scholarships, one for a boy and one for a girl. So from early in life I learnt that the only option I should focus on was being number one. The result was that I won the parish scholarship.

Concurrently, in the same year, astounding to both me and everyone else, I passed the Third Jamaica Local Examination, in spite of the circumstances that attended my preparation and my relatively young age.

I was the only student in St. Thomas to pass the third exam that year. I was also now familiar with the *Gazette* and knew how to look for my name.

I had a passion to become a teacher. The Third Jamaica Local Examination qualified me for entry into the prestigious and noble institution, The Mico, which had a reputation then of being the "poor man's university," with a diverse blend of students from every strata of society.

The University of the West Indies (UWI) and the University of Technology (UTECH), formerly the College of Arts Science and Technology (CAST), were then newly established and fledgling institutions of higher learning, compared to The Mico, which began operations in 1836.

Regrettably, I was too young for admission to The Mico. The parish scholarship qualified me, however, to enter Dinthill Technical High School, which turned out to be a most opportune move and an auspicious beginning to my post-elementary school education.

My high school years at Dinthill were a profound character-building leg of my life's journey. It was there that I experienced and developed a heightened self-awareness, self-understanding, knowledge of my own strengths and weaknesses, intrapersonal skills, and leadership capacity.

Generally, Dinthill facilitated an all-around dynamic and amazing learning and growth experience for me.

It was in high school that I became truly conscious of the value and importance of leadership. It was then that I began to develop an interest in the concept of leadership, and become more active and reflective in the pursuit of my leadership potential.

The Dinthill school's community of educators and others provided the requisite support and commitment, utilizing intentional and creative

Time Management

approaches, and pursued vigorously the leadership development of all who were interested in being so developed.

Time management is one of the first important life-skill and leadership lessons that I learnt at Dinthill.

Leadership Lesson

Time management is an important part of your toolkit as a leader.

In my time Dinthill was a boarding school for boys. On a typical weekday, the day began at 4:00 a.m. for those who were on dairy duty. The cows had to be taken from the pasture at Deeside to the station to be milked.

This was important because the milk was for breakfast for everyone. Hence, each boy in the dormitory would make sure that the person(s) on dairy duty were up on time and off to the task in good time.

This was particularly rough stuff because Linstead, where the school is located, was, at that time of the morning back then, dark, cold, and heavy with fog, with very low visibility.

I recall an amusing incident when one of the boys on dairy duty, who was hurrying to get dressed in the semidarkness of the early morning dormitory, complained bitterly that someone, or all of us, had sewn up the fly of his briefs/underpants.

While each of us, and all of us, were quite capable of getting up to such mischief, we were not the culprits. As it turned out—and as he discovered when the lights came on, much to his embarrassment—he had, in the dark, mistakenly put on his underwear backward!

If you were lucky to be placed on other morning duties, such as cutting the grass, trimming trees, picking oranges from the orchard or tomatoes from the farm, or collecting eggs for breakfast, your day would start at 6:00 a.m.

After the special early morning duties, the regular daily schedule for all was as follows:

Breakfast at 7:00 a.m., cadet parade at 7:45 a.m., morning devotion at 8:00 a.m., classes or work on the farm from 8:30 a.m. to noon.

If you worked on the farm in the morning, you would attend classes in the afternoon, and vice-versa; hence, the following schedule:

Lunch from 12:00 to1:00 p.m., classes or work on the farm from 1:00 to 4:30 p.m., sports practice and/or cadet training from 4:30 to 5:30 p.m., shower from 5:30 to 6:00 p.m., supper from 6:00 to 7:00 p.m., compulsory prep/study period from 7:00 to 8:45 p.m., evening devotion from 8:45 to 9:00 p.m., and lights out/bedtime at 9:30 p.m.

Talk about a packed day! We longed for weekends!

On weekends, we were to organize our own amusement.

Parties were frequently held, where we grooved to the latest pop music and showed off our dance moves.

Concerts were another favourite, where we gathered to showcase our talents.

Movies were yet another popular recreational activity. We rented the films from Palace Amusement Company in Kingston. This activity afforded me an exciting diversion. As the chief operator of the school's projector, I had the privilege of travelling by train to Kingston on a Saturday morning and renting movies like *Student Prince* to show at school in the evening.

Weekends were also the time to participate in club activities and attend the church service of our choice.

We would periodically, on some weekends, have cadet retreats in the capital town of different parishes. The girls would call us "young soldiers" as we marched through the respective town on a Saturday morning.

Later in the evening, we hoped that we would meet some of them at the party organized for us, which we all looked forward to attending.

A very important follow-up to these cadet retreats was the critical follow-on letter from one of the girls you met at the party. Such a letter could make or break your manhood, your "swag," and your all-important reputation as a "girls' man."

To not get this vital piece of correspondence from a girl was, to our juvenile minds, to suffer a fate worse than death for the hapless *unfortunate* boy—cruel and unrelenting *ridicule*!

To avoid the torturous ridicule of his peers, a boy—unsure or definitely certain that a "legitimate" letter from a girl might or definitely *would not* be forthcoming—would make sure that a letter by fair means or foul would arrive nonetheless.

Such a boy would have learnt the subtle art of writing a letter to himself and, through a great deal of subterfuge and conspiracy with a nameless conspirator, would arrange to have such a letter mailed from the town where the cadet retreat had been held.

The said letter would then arrive at the school, legitimately through the mail, and the boy's pride and "mojo" were effectively established.

Creative and strategic thinking at its best!

Self-Reliance

The second leadership lesson I learnt as a student at Dinthill was the importance of *self-reliance*.

At Dinthill we were taught to appreciate and practice the principle of "Eat what you grow and grow what you eat."

At Dinthill, we, the students, worked the farm. In addition to taking care of the livestock, we also tended the crops. We planted yams, potatoes, tomatoes, and other vegetables. It was these crops that we reaped that enriched our hearty and healthy menus. We truly "ate what we grew and grew what we ate."

This "Eat what you grow..." principle was instituted and reinforced as part of the school's curriculum and social ethos. It has within it the important element of self-reliance, which is a key objective of empowering people.

beliefs / aspirations

Servant Leadership Lesson

Servant leadership must involve the objective of self-reliance as a key building block for empowering the persons being served.

Over the years I have observed how self-reliance became a key pillar in our quest for national sustainable development.

Evidence of this is that one of the significant rallying cries of the democratic socialism approach to governance in the 1970s was self-reliance.

In that era, the government urged Jamaicans to grow the economy and reduce economic drain, by curbing their appetite for foreign goods, and end the reliance on imported food products.

The national campaign then—"Eat what we grow and grow what we eat"—sought to engage the citizens and encourage their interest in the benefits of farming solutions in order to propel Jamaica toward greater self-reliance in food production and consumption.

The campaign also sought to promote agriculture as a viable and mutually beneficial socioeconomic enterprise.

In more recent times, the slogan has once again become a clarion call for national food security, which is of critical importance for Jamaica as a small, developing island state.

The lesson of self-reliance and its correlation to leadership is obvious when one considers that the word "leading" means being out-front... trailblazing, leading by example, and developing followers who have initiative, persistence, and determination.

The lessons of self-reliance I garnered from the experience of growing the food we ate at Dinthill continue to resonate in the character of my leadership.

Jan Rutherford, founder of Self-Reliant Leadership, captures one of the critical underpinnings of my leadership character when she says, "One of the most important components of our own personal development is the desire to build our character to serve other sinner growth for outer service."

My high school years at Dinthill were truly powerful and impactful.

Throughout our experiences, in and out of the classroom, we were constantly learning new and exciting skills, and being shaped as leaders. We were taught to take responsibility, develop good habits, and become self-reliant.

Holistic Education

Beyond self-reliance, however, there is another very important lesson I learnt from the agricultural enterprise at Dinthill that is worth sharing with you.

Servant Leadership Lesson

Holistic education is an effective model for leadership development and practice.

The combination of the core subjects, English and mathematics, in tandem with technical vocational subjects and cocurricular activities to facilitate experiential learning is a dynamic and excellent recipe for holistic education.

True to its name, holistic education places an emphasis on the *whole* growth and development of the learner, instead of emphasizing only specific parts of the education experience.

The positive results of Dinthill's multidimensional, well-balanced, holistic education and training is deeply embedded in my leadership character to date.

An interesting example of the result and value of holistic development can be garnered from the Dinthill memories of one of my schoolmates, Lloyd Delpratt.

Lloyd's encounter with then principal Roy C. Gayle is recounted in full detail as follows:

> As second-year students, five of us were assigned to work in the horticultural plot. If someone said, "R. C. is coming!" that meant the principal was heading in our direction.
>
> On this particular day, when the warning was sounded that "R. C. is coming!" he was not only heading in our direction, but he also came directly to us, which was threateningly unusual.

Suddenly I knew why when he asked the question, "Which one of you students has been playing the piano in the wee hours of the morning?"

I faced him and said, "It's me, sir."

He then said, "Meet me in my office in ten minutes!"

My world started to crumble under my feet as I stood in his office thinking the worst. I thought that perhaps the old gentleman living on the boundary line of our property, facing the main road, must have heard me and brought my misdemeanor to the attention of the principal. I was nervous with anxiety.

R. C. looked up at me, graciously offered me a seat, and said, "Do you like to play the piano?"

I said, "Yes sir."

With that little verbal exchange, I somehow began to feel more at ease, and the sense of foreboding was fast receding.

You see, I knew that R. C. was a musician who played the piano for us at school many times and also played the organ at his church. So I felt in that moment a sense of kinship with him, and, as a fellow musician, he would be kind to me.

I recalled that in my first year, I was able to convince the head prefect, Lloyd Stanley, that I was compellingly drawn to music, and I needed his permission to go to the graduating class's dance to listen to the music of the Berty King Orchestra from Kingston.

I thought too of another senior student, Carl McCloud, who

taught me to play the tenor drums in the Cadet Band while he played the snare drums beside me.

Memories like those that flashed through my mind as I faced the principal in his office emboldened me to expect and face any reprieve or reprimand R. C. might choose to deliver.

I was therefore cool and calm, though quite relieved, when he said to me, "Delpratt, I am giving you permission to play the piano after classes, except for special events."

I all but saluted the good man as I rose from the seat, stood at attention, and respectfully said, "Thank you, sir," before leaving his office.

I am eternally grateful to Mr. R. C. Gayle and the Dinthill community of staff and students, who encouraged and facilitated the development of my musical abilities which led to a very successful and highly satisfying career in music.

Graduates from Dinthill in that era had outstanding careers after graduation in a wide variety of fields in Jamaica and internationally—university professors, teachers, ministers of religion, architects, engineers, farmers, accountants, economists, hotel managers, management consultants, librarians, corporate executives, human resource practitioners, sports administrators, musicians, and other professionals.

In fact, Lloyd Delpratt became the organist and keyboard specialist for the Vikings Band, one of Jamaica's top bands in the 1960s. Also named in his story, Carl McCloud became Jamaica's top jazz drummer; and Lloyd Stanley became a human resources development consultant.

Unquestionably, the value and impact of holistic education as we

Negotiation

received at Dinthill is in large measure responsible for much of the success of its past students.

Another important leadership skill I developed at Dinthill was the art and science of negotiation.

I was elected head boy and appointed cadet quarter master sergeant (CQMS), both of which immediately led to my first challenging experience as a high school leader.

At eight thirty one evening, during compulsory prep/study time, our principal, R. C. Gayle, gathered the entire student body to make an important announcement.

The "headline" of the announcement was peculiar but not at all unusual for R. C. Gayle and his audience.

"Gentlemen, Dennis is dead!" he deadpanned.

Principal Gayle was known for dramatic opening statements in his address at assembly every Monday morning.

His presentations were always rich with valuable takeaways of wisdom and advice on how we should live our lives, take advantage of opportunities, and spend our time productively, among other gems.

My classmate C. K. Robinson recalled, and would remind me of, the many dramatic opening statements our principal was given to making in his Monday morning presentations.

One such legendary announcement was pronounced the Monday following Jamaica's tragic train crash at Kendall. The principal's opening statement then was "Derailment leads to fatality!"

Lascelles Dixon, one of my schoolmates at Dinthill (who became an outstanding architect), recalled the following story about one of our principal's inspiring speeches.

> Having just returned from his visit to London, our principal, Mr. R. C. Gayle, decided that he would share his experience with the usual Monday morning gathering of students. In sharing his London experience, he spoke about the smog. He zeroed in on the details of the smog as follows:
>
> "When that smog descends and lodges upon your head and hands, it is like thick snow...You can see just a few feet before you. One can hardly breathe, it is stifling. Sometimes people bump into each other..."
>
> He took a good look at those students in the audience who were soon to graduate and said to them, "You must see this institution called Dinthill as a stepping-stone!
>
> Some of you will be going on to the Jamaica School of Agriculture (JSA), some to Mico College, some to the College of Arts Science and Technology (CAST), and others to the world of work.
>
> Wherever you may go and whatever you may do, <u>beware of the smog of complacency</u>!...It can stifle you and cripple your vision of the future."
>
> For those of us who heard this charge, it reverberated deep down in our souls like a church bell does, even to this day.

Now back to the "Dennis Is Dead" episode...

When the principal announced that "Dennis is dead" with seemingly deadly seriousness, we were immediately plunged into deep shock and sorrow as we sought to come to grips with the news about the passing of our student colleague, Dennis.

Having led off with the sensational headline to grab his audience's attention, the principal continued in true broadcasting style to provide us with further details.

In sum, he recounted the story of his return journey to the campus that night from the Anglican Church in Bog Walk, where he had gone for choir practice (he was an excellent tenor). His headlights shone on Dennis escorting a young lady from evening class.

Like a deer caught in the headlights, Dennis was stricken. The principal was also, given the circumstances, mortified!

To be seen in the company of a female—alone and unchaperoned by an authorized adult beyond boundaries and school time—was a grave offense, which mortally imperiled Dennis's continued tenure at the school.

In short, the principal announced, Dennis would be expelled forthwith!

The antecedent story of Dennis's death comes against the background of the Ministry of Education, which gave the school permission to offer evening classes to all who qualified for attendance—including girls from the community.

This permission was granted under the ministry's strict orders that the boys who were officially enrolled at the school as full-time students would not mix with the part-time students attending evening classes, and especially not with the young ladies!

The thought of Dennis's expulsion was very unsettling to me. The extremely harsh punishment did not seem to me to fit the crime. So disquieted I was that the following day I requested a meeting with the principal.

Being head boy carried with it a certain status and special privileges, such as a favourable response to the request for a "consultation" with the principal (the subtle message being to the student body that "the head boy run tings!").

The request for a meeting approved, I proceeded to the principal's office to plead Dennis's mercy on the court.

In making my appeal, I asked the judge/principal for clémency [lenience] on Dennis's behalf. I also asked that he give due consideration to affording Dennis an opportunity for redemption, rather than outright expulsion.

I had prepared my case and my arguments well, in anticipation of any counterarguments the "honourable" judge/principal might proffer.

After a rather intense and lengthy "trial," involving many grueling and dueling arguments on both sides, the judge/principal relented and a decision was made. Dennis would be allowed, and was now free, to remain in school—on one condition:

The judge/principal sternly pronounced, "You must make sure Dennis does not get into any other mischief, and if he does, I will expel both of you!"

That was a charge I could not afford to forfeit!

I am happy to report that Dennis stayed the course and walked on the path of the straight and narrow, without further incidence of misbehaviour throughout his remaining school years.

It was a very proud moment when, together, we both successfully graduated from the institution. At graduation, I also received the coveted Chairman's Prize for Outstanding Leadership.

Long before graduation, however, I had bagged, what was to me then as a student, an even more valued prize: the respect and admiration of my peers for standing up for Dennis and boldly challenging, respectfully, the principal's decision.

I didn't know it then, but coming out of my comfort zone, standing up for a principle, and taking a personal risk is one of the hallmarks of a transformational leader.

During the month of December each year, all of us as young men of Dinthill were privileged to visit the neighbouring Carron Hall, an all-girl institution, and together as students, we would enjoy an annual Christmas party.

This much-anticipated event was an occasion for us young men to, first and foremost, catch the attention and win the affection of the lovely young ladies. As peacocks would plume their feathers, we boys would show off our skills at singing and dancing to impress the ladies and win their admiration.

One year, my classmate Pablo Nugent and I sang the popular "All I Have to Do Is Dream" by the Everly Brothers. This was a hit and set the mood for the party.

Alas, when the party was in full swing at 9:00 p.m., it was time to stop the music, dim the lights, and bring an end to the fun. Of course, we did not want to leave, so the boys asked me to negotiate an extra hour with our principal, who was of course our chaperone for the night.

I duly met with the principal and, with some persuasion, got his tacit agreement to extend the party for an hour, pending the further agreement of the principal of Carron Hall. Together they agreed to the extension until 10:00 p.m. It goes without saying that my "stock" rose among my peers!

One important spin-off benefit from these parties was the development of my literary and writing skills. In those days we had no cell phones or social media, so we had to rely on written communication.

The Sunday after the party we would spend hours in the library researching choice quotations from classic writers, such as Shakespeare and Emily Bronte, to include in our special love letters/compositions to the girls we hoped would remember us with great affection. (By the way, our teachers thought that we were very studious students.)

A young lady then would admire you based on your literary skills and your "lyrical stylings." These were important steps toward developing my mastery of written communication skills.

All these lessons were invaluable to me later in life, personally and professionally.

At every stage of my growth and development, I have been shaped as a leader—in the home, church, community, school, and elsewhere.

While I have been personally rewarded in so many ways for the development of my leadership potential, particularly during the significant high school years, it is my hope that the societal benefits of my leadership are far greater, more far-reaching, and more impactful than any benefit to me.

I have chosen to share the close of this chapter on my high school years and the many leadership lessons from my experiences, encounters, and exposures, with a few words from Dr. Suzanne Bean, director, Roger F. Wicker Center for Creative Learning:

> Broaden students' concept of leadership by helping them understand that authentic leadership has more to do with influence than who holds an appointed position, or who is popular, or who has the best grades, or who has the most money.

And from my own thoughts…

Servant Leadership Lessons

Lesson 1: *The art and science of negotiation is an important part of your toolkit as a leader.*

Lesson 2: *To be successful in attempting transformative initiatives, there are critical points of time in your life when you have to be brave and come out of your comfort zone and do things you have never done before.*

5

Empowering the Servant Leader:
Stories, Lessons, and Impact of the Collegiate Level

> Certain leadership skills and attributes
> are best developed before you get out into the professional world,
> and that is what makes college a great place
> to develop these qualities.
> —Pat Fredshaw

COLLEGE IS AN absolutely amazing experience in any young person's journey through life.

It is truly a wonderful opportunity to explore and discover new knowledge and ideas…unearth and unleash new and latent passions, skills, and talents…develop deeper self-awareness and confidence… and build and <u>establish powerful lifelong relationships and connections</u> with far-reaching impact.

Admission to Mico College was one of my early aspirations. This desire and ambition was further driven and reinforced by the influence of my elementary school teacher, Mr. Jarrett, and my headmaster, D.R.B. Grant, who were both illustrious Miconians.

My sights were somewhat dimmed by the veil of doubt cast over my "vision" by my neighbour Alton Lawson (of blessed memory), who was a probationer at my elementary school.

Mr. Lawson told me how difficult it was to get into The Mico. He said that he had sat for the entrance examination no less than two times… without success.

The second time that he sat for the examination, he was told that he placed thirty-first. But regrettably, they were only selecting thirty students. The exact response, which was seared painfully in his memory, was "We only need thirty students and you are number thirty-one!"

According to his recount of the story to me, then principal of The Mico, the legendary A. J. Newman, popularly known as "Ceps," told him that he was "next in line."

He proceeded, therefore, to sit for the entrance exam a third time and succeeded in making the grade for admission into the venerable and distinguished Mico, where he went on to become a star student.

At Dinthill, my former high school, I was a member of the track team. One day, while I was on my way to the track for warm-up before a race, I heard an important news item over the radio (Radio Jamaica and Redifusion, now called RJR).

The news was that The Mico would be offering an increased number of full scholarships. Each of these scholarships would cover tuition fees, accommodations, and textbooks.

I was now even more motivated to send in my application to The Mico.

I abandoned track training that afternoon in favour of devoting the time to start studying for The Mico entrance examination.

Thanks to my neighbour Alton Lawson, who had informed me of the areas covered in the entrance examination, I knew where to focus my studying.

I duly applied, sat for the requisite first entrance examination, and placed in the top six! It was with a great deal of pride and a keen sense of accomplishment that I accepted the offer of admission to The Mico.

The Mico then had two entrance examinations. The first was to select the number of students they needed and in addition five more persons. If you made it successfully to this select group, you would then pursue a pre-college course in English, Latin, and mathematics for one year.

One year later, the second entrance examinations followed the pre-college course and were conducted on a Monday and Tuesday. On Friday morning of the same week, you returned for the results.

Should you be successful, you went on from there, on the said Friday afternoon, to the doctor for "medicals." All being well with the medical results, you reported to college the following day, Saturday afternoon.

Great turnaround time for the entire process from examination to results and enrollment!

The painful part of the exercise for some people, and uncomfortable for all of us, however, was that when the results were announced, only the names of those who were *unsuccessful* were called out, and they were asked to leave immediately.

The names were called out by the famous Arthur Grant (grandfather of Kathy Moss and Elizabeth Ward). Pythie, as he was affectionately called (short for Pythagoras, the famous Greek mathematician and philosopher), would later be my lecturer in mathematics and Latin at The Mico.

This announcement of examination results was a very unnerving experience for all of us, and particularly devastating for the ones who were unsuccessful and had to suffer the public humiliation (though that was not The Mico's intent) of having their names publicly broadcasted.

I recall well those people who were not successful and who, unfortunately, had sat in the front of Classroom B, where the results were announced. They had the burden of getting up and making the seemingly long walk of shame and pain, from the front of the room to the exit door at the back of the room.

You can imagine the absolute distress of those students, many of whom would have been joyously celebrated with a royal send-off by their family and members of their community, prior to coming to this final entrance examination.

I give thanks that I was successful on the first attempt.

Over the years, The Mico has undergone expansion and development, both physically and in its academic programmes, but the philosophy and core values that underpin and drives its ethos, however it may be worded, is constant.

The Mico philosophy is as follows:

"The Mico is committed to the promotion of personal growth, and development of all its constituents and nation building.

As an institution that embraces student-centeredness, we are committed to providing our students with the highest quality education through a holistic learning environment which encourages research and scholarship, and which nurtures and prepares them with the requisite knowledge, skills, competencies, morals, and values to be transformational leaders in an ever-changing complex world."

The Mico has four core values – Leadership , Service to others , Integrity and Excellence in Performance:

"Leadership—We are committed to developing and nurturing ethical and value-based individuals who will exert positive influence and be agents of transformative changes in whatever institution and community they serve."

"Service to Others—We are committed to the practice of service for the well-being and improved quality of life of others through habits of empathy, caring, empowerment, civic and social responsibility."

"Integrity—We are committed to developing individuals who demonstrate the ethical attributes of honesty, fair play, trustworthiness, and respect for self and others."

"Excellence in Performance—We are committed to developing critical thinkers who consistently display creativity and innovativeness for achieving the highest standards of performance."

The philosophy of The Mico and its four core values are fundamental to my own beliefs as a person and have become a fundamental part of my character as a leader. They have helped me to grow and develop personally and professionally.

They form the foundation on which I perform work and conduct myself, and they are the driving forces that have shaped and marked my leadership.

Indeed, my passion for service is a deeply held belief that had long been instilled and grounded in me, through teaching and practice, by my mother and others in my early years.

The Mico, however, further deepened, heightened, and defined this quality more clearly. The significant influence of The Mico's core value in principle and practice of "service for the well-being and improved quality of life of others..." underpins and guides everything I do, and it is given the highest priority in all my undertakings.

The Mico's holistic learning environment required all students, as part of our programme of studies, to participate in clubs, societies, and the many opportunities for social outreach activities.

One of these was the Jamaica 4-H Club, which has, as its mission statement, "To mobilize, educate, and train youth in agricultural and related skills through the effective deployment of staff and volunteers, utilizing adaptive technologies to influence trainees to develop sustainable enterprises and become positive contributors to national development."

I entered The Mico with some experience in this area as a former president of the 4-H Club at my high school, Dinthill.

One day each week, we had to visit a community to help community members form and establish their own 4-H Club, engage in activities for their own personal development, and make positive contributions to their community.

These 4-H Club experiences were enhanced by two "leading lights."

The first was Winston Wright (affectionately called Rabbi). He was a third-year student when I entered The Mico and had vast experience as a 4-H Club president and a leader in other areas.

He was instrumental in the selection of schools and the activities I had designed for and would coordinate with them. He was generous in sharing his wealth of knowledge and experience with me, and I garnered from him much useful information on organizing 4-H Club activities at the school and wider community level.

The second leading light in the 4-H Club movement was Renford Shirley, He was a "grub lecturer," which was an affectionate title for faculty members who started teaching the year after we entered The Mico.

Mr. Shirley was an excellent lecturer in teaching methods. In addition, he was both knowledgeable and passionate about the Jamaica 4-H Clubs movement. He was so passionate in this effort that sometimes we had differences of opinion about whether my classes in mathematics were more important than 4-H Club activities!

Sometimes on my way to math classes, he would approach me saying, "Ying, remember the 4-H club meeting!"

His interest in my holistic development and his endearing personality inspired me to strike the balance, however, and arrive at a mutually satisfying resolution to the issue. So mathematics and 4-H Clubs grew side by side and apace!

At The Mico, our music group was led by our music lecturer, Olive Lewin, who later became the Honourable Dr. Olive Lewin OD, OM—Jamaican author, social anthropologist, musicologist, and teacher.

She is best known for her recorded anthologies of old Jamaican folk songs, researched and collected over her lifetime. She is also highly regarded for her role as founder and director of the renowned and widely acclaimed Jamaica Folk Singers.

Olive Lewin's eminent distinction in the arts was as apparent to us then as it is now acknowledged and celebrated locally and internationally. The Mico community benefited tremendously from her outstanding abilities.

Through music, she engaged us in dynamic social outreach activities. One of these activities was to "bring good cheer through singing" to persons with mental illness at the Bellevue Hospital.

One incident I vividly recall occurred after our performance of a particular piece. One of the patients would not stop cheering in a very loud voice. When the nurse tried to stop him, he loudly exclaimed, "This is a madhouse; we must make noise!"

What was touching and sobering about this event was that I recognized this gentleman as the former head of the Government Tax Office in my hometown.

I always had a great empathy and sympathy for people with mental health problems. My first direct engagement with persons afflicted by mental illness was at a young age.

One of my many tasks while growing up was to help my mother take care of one of her cousins who was mentally ill. He had developed a paranoia that someone was coming to hurt him.

It was deeply disturbing and emotionally painful to me, as a young child, to see this big man in size and status reduced to cowering and trembling, and trying to hide behind a very small door (relative to his large frame) whenever he was experiencing one of his episodes.

When those episodes occurred, his wife could not handle the situation, so my mother would be called to help. Over time he came to live with us.

My job each day—before school in the morning, at lunch break, and after school in the evenings—was to go to his former home, deliver his dirty clothes to his wife for her to launder, and then collect from her the meal that she had prepared for him, as well as a clean set of clothes.

What I found fascinating was that when he was not having these episodes of paranoia, he would engage me in very high-level intellectual discussions, for he was a well-educated man.

From my relationship with him, the big takeaway lesson for me was that spending quality time to help people with problems is good therapy for them and you.

Continuing with stories from The Mico and my experience with Olive Lewin in music and Wycliffe Bennett in speech and drama...

I was also part of The Mico's first Operetta, Barbarina, a simple adaptation of the Marriage of Figaro by Mozart because I had a combination of skills in each of the areas required- speech, drama and singing.

This operetta was produced and directed by Olive Lewin, our lecturer in music, and Wycliffe Bennett, our lecturer in speech and drama, who in later years became chairman emeritus of the Ward Theatre Foundation; life member of the Little Theatre Movement; general manager of the Jamaica Broadcasting Corporation; chairman of the Creative Production and Training Centre (CPTC), the Jamaica School of Drama, and the Jamaica School of Music; and a fellow of the Woodrow Wilson International Center for Scholars.

The operetta was staged at The Mico, on the lawns of Quebec Lodge, which was then the official residence of the principal of the college.

I have fond memories of Quebec Lodge.

I was not an art specialist, but I must have had some gifts in that area, or perhaps it might have been the influence of the artist and intellectual, with whom I closely interacted in my home environs, early in my life.

The result was that my drawing of this building was considered "good enough," by the discriminating examiners, to enable me to do well in my art examination.

The piece was entitled "An Artistic Impression Using Mathematical Shapes." This was so because I envisaged buildings as a creative embodiment of squares, rectangles, triangles, and circles.

In *Babarina*, my batch mates and I played most of the lead roles. Esther Bryan played the role of Barbarina; Walter Subadan was Figaro; Daisy Graham, Susanna; and I played the role of Servant to the Count. Dennis Watson, who was my senior in high school at Dinthill, and again my senior in college at The Mico, played the role of Cherubino.

The remaining cast included outstanding students such as Vivian Crawford, Henry Sterling, Albert Neufville, Barbara Llewellyn, Sylvia Edwards, Norma Ellis, Owen James, Herman Saunders, Lloyd Patrick, Desmond Chambers and Michael Mitchell, who all played the roles of villagers and members of the choir during different scenes of the operetta.

In addition to singing, they also inserted improvised comments that were definitely not part of the script. Fortunately, only those of us on stage could hear clearly what they were saying.

In the audience was our English lecturer, Miss Duncan, who would use any and every occasion to grade our language competencies and let us know the grade after the performance. So it certainly would not do for her to hear what was being said by these villagers.

An unplanned and amusing incident happened during the performance of the operetta.

Immediately after Barbarina said "How late is he now", the clock in the Buxton Tower of the College started striking 8 o'clock in the evening.

This resulted in spontaneous laughter by the audience and members of the cast.

The operetta was a huge success.

The article in our daily newspaper, the Gleaner. of April 7, 1960 confirms this. This article "Introducing students to the music of Mozart" was written by Peter Dawson (the pen name for Pam Ogorman, Director of the School of Music, which is now part of the Edna Manley College of the Visual and Performing Arts}.

The following is an excerpt from this article:

"This was not an occasion for criticism, rather must one commend Miss Olive Lewin and Mr Wycliffe Bennett and all concerned for this initiative. Not only did it involve the selection of students with some acting ability but also the selection of students who, with young untrained voices would have the courage to sing on stage."

The day after the staging of the operetta, a young lady from Shortwood Teachers' College called me to congratulate The Mico on staging this event and me on my performance. She requested a meeting with me, as an executive of The Mico Drama Club, to discuss how Shortwood could stage a similar production.

She offered to visit with me at The Mico, the preferred venue for the proposed meeting.

At that stage of life, young male students like me were not yet influenced by the famous lines from one of the more memorable songs in the operetta: "Now your days of philandering are over and your roaming from flower to flower, you will no more as a great Casanova play Adonis to each pretty maid."

Naturally, I agreed to her visit with me.

The young lady, as it turned out, was quite a beauty—an extremely attractive young lady and very much the "head-turner." Her visit with me on campus, at Mills Hall, caused quite a stir. I later learnt that a big part of the excitement, beyond her good looks, stemmed from another student's false boast that *she came to visit him!*

The fact was that the young lady had only approached him in the lobby and asked him to call Neville Ying for her!

The truth of the matter was eventually revealed, as all truths are wont to do, and he got quite a ribbing from the men in Mills Hall for his troubles. I, in turn, got quite the applause for the fine young lady's visit with me.

My social profile and popularity soared sky high!

In addition to my involvement with the operetta, I was also an active participant in other music, speech, and drama activities.

In the field of music, I was one of the lead bass singers in the Mico College Choir and one member of a quartet that participated in the Nathan Brisettt Music Competition.

Rupert Burey sang tenor in the Mico College Choir. He was my batch mate and, like me, a member of the Mathematics Specialist Group. More importantly, Rupert was my friend.

It was Rupert who helped me to get a job during the Christmas holidays at one of the Hanna Stores on King Street in downtown Kingston. My holiday work with the Hanna Store chain provided a good opportunity for a powerful introduction to the business sector.

The Hanna Store on King Street, where I worked, was called GEM. The store specialized in a variety of items with particular appeal to young ladies. From my earnings, I bought a young lady I had eyes on a lovely powder dish with a raised, sculpted mermaid forming the cover.

It was my friend Rupert who lent me his new transistor radio to help me entertain the same young lady when I took her on a visit to Hope Gardens.

There being no further details on that special outing, I move on…

In the area of speech and drama, Wycliffe Bennett would make us practice projecting our voices. He would do so by having us practice speaking in the open air, in well-modulated tones, at a point in the playing field. He would sit in the Sports Pavilion about fifty yards away to assess if you could be heard clearly, without shouting.

During these practice sessions I would do select pieces, such as Abraham Lincoln's famous speech at Gettysburg. "Four score and seven years ago our fathers brought forth on this continent, a new nation, conceived in liberty, and dedicated to the proposition that all men are created equal…"

An amusing incident occurred when I recited one of these pieces inside a building for the first time. It was at a speech and drama competitions held in the St. Andrew High School Auditorium.

When I opened by mouth and delivered the first line, the entire audience reacted with great alarm. It turned out that the already high volume of the speakers had further amplified the naturally booming timbre of my voice, accentuated even further by the speech coach ministrations of Wycliffe Bennett with all his insistence on "Project! Project!"

The resulting frighteningly thunderous roar—which seemed not to belong to the figure on stage, given my small frame—descended on the unarmed ears of the hapless audience like the prophetic "trumpet call" of the biblical end times.

The audience was unprepared. The auditorium shook...as much by the unexpected volume as by the quality of the delivery. The group I led for this speech competition *won!*

I also enjoyed other selections, such as sections of the poem "Helen of Troy" by Christopher Marlowe:

> Was this the face that launched a thousand ship<u>s</u>
> And burned the topless towers of Illium?
> Sweet Helen, make me immortal with a kiss:
> Her lips suck forth my soul, see where it flies.
> Come Helen, come, give me my soul again.
> Here will I dwell, for heaven be in these lips."

The third through sixth stanzas helped me to shape my lyrics to attract the attention of young ladies. For instance, I replaced the name "Helen" in the poem with the name of a young lady of interest—"Esther."

But there were also musical items in which I performed that brought me down to earth about the effectiveness of my lyrics and how not to interpret incorrectly the signals and actions from young ladies. An example of this is the following selection from John Barlet*:*

> When from my love I looked for love
> And kind affection's due,
> Too well I found her vows to prove
> Most faithless and untrue;
>
> For when I did ask her why,
> Most sharply she did reply
> That she with me did ne'er agree
> To love but jestingly.
>
> Mark the subtle policies
> That female lovers find,
> Who loves to fix their constancies
> Like feathers in the wind;

Though they swear, vow, and protest
That they love you chiefly best,
Yet by-and-by they'll all deny,
And say 'twas but in jest.

These were important lessons to learn at that stage of life as a young man.

Participation in music, speech, and drama performances and competitions, together with teaching practicum experiences, taught me important leadership lessons.

Leadership Lessons

Lesson 1: *As a leader it is important that you demonstrate that you value the importance of preparation and research.*

Lesson 2: *As a leader, when you make oral presentations, pay particular attention to being audible, articulate, compelling, and correct in grammar and pronunciation.*

Many years later, I found these two leadership lessons and the skills embedded in them to be invaluable in the delivery of a wide range of oral presentations I had to make to diverse audiences locally, regionally, and internationally.

In addition to the opportunities provided by The Mico for participation in activities in the arts and other fields, I also sought out and participated in many other activities off campus during the holidays.

I joined the Ivy Baxter Dance Group in my hometown of Morant Bay, for instance.

Ivy Baxter was an epic Jamaican woman. She is best known for her pioneering work in promoting creative dance, and dance theatre in communities.

My involvement with the Ivy Baxter Dance Troupe led to my performing a dance routine with her troupe from Morant Bay at the annual Denbigh Show in Clarendon.

According to the Jamaica Agricultural Society (JAS), under whose auspices the Denbigh show is held, "The Denbigh Show is the oldest, largest, and most dynamic agricultural show in the English-speaking Caribbean, and one of Jamaica's most iconic events, dating back to its introduction in 1952. It is Jamaica and the Caribbean's premier agricultural event and epitomizes 'wholesome family entertainment'."

Denbigh would attract thousands of people to the event annually. For me to be afforded the opportunity to perform on such a nationally significant platform, to such a large and diverse audience, was indeed a *big deal*.

Interestingly, many years later, on an occasion at the Pegasus Hotel, I met the young lady who was my dance partner in the routine we performed at Denbigh, and whom I had not seen in years since she migrated to the USA.

I reminded her of our dancing at Denbigh. She excitedly called her children and grandchildren over to where we were talking and asked me to repeat the story to them.

They seemed to have had this notion, and displayed the attitude, that their mom and grandma did not know anything about dancing.

I made her day by recalling this event and serving as a "witness" to her lively and exciting past, rich with memories of her dancing prowess.

Another off-campus activity in which I was engaged was dance classes.

St. Joseph's Teachers' College was an all-female institution that would regularly host parties to which I was invited and would attend. They also had a Latin dance class, conducted by Clive Thompson, dancer extraordinaire and choreographer of distinction. I joined the class and made the cha-cha my speciality.

At the end of the series of classes, there was a cha-cha competition, in which my dance partner and I were duly entered. Together we "cha-cha-ed" our way to winning!

My partner was an especially attractive young lady from North Clarendon, who was also a student at St Joseph's. Needless to say, I was more than a little smitten by her appeal as a potential romantic partner, rather than as a dance partner. We may have won the dance competition together, but I, regrettably, did not win her heart.

Photography was another extracurricular activity that captured my interest and attention. I was president of The Mico Photography Club.

I recall with wry amusement how my fellow photographer and classmate, Bill Brown, and I would focus our lens on another dimension of photography, beyond the camera.

We would, on any given Saturday afternoon, suit up in "decent clothes," our cameras strategically slung over our shoulders, and off we would go to attend, quite uninvited, select weddings in Kingston and St. Andrew.

As the presumed wedding photographers, we would be the first to be served drinks and a special meal. This especially hearty fare satisfied our main interest and desire, and more than adequately justified the great lengths to which we would go to secure a free meal.

Jamaicans are renowned for their generous culinary expression of hospitality, especially on special occasions like a wedding, and we knew our appetites would not be disappointed.

As college students, food was always a high-priority need, especially on weekends. My partner in crime, Bill Brown, and I thought it was ingenious to combine both our skill in photography and our need for good food by being wedding crashers.

Truth is, we did, quite honestly, take photographs and hone our skills in photography at the same time. But the whole truth and nothing but the truth is that we knew none of the couples, nor their party!

College is truly a great time to develop your confidence and a healthy belief in yourself and your abilities, without which you will never be able to succeed as a leader. I clearly must have had more than my fair share of confidence to have conceptualized and so successfully and consistently pulled off those wedding photography escapades.

Upon reflection, what was interesting about my involvement in all those extracurricular activities, on and off campus, while a student at The Mico was that it did not contribute to my grade point average (GPA) at all! That was not my motivation, but it certainly contributed big time to the development of important life skills.

It is my firmly held belief that it is of critical importance that all students—at whatever level, but in particular at the collegiate level—must extend themselves to take advantage of the rich and dynamic experience of a holistic learning environment, such as the one The Mico provides.

It is vital that they do so in order to develop the much-needed self-awareness, self-confidence, and ability to identify and display effective communication and interpersonal and other skills students will need in all spheres of their lives, and particularly in leadership.

I also believe strongly that schooling, at all levels, should provide leadership development opportunities for students.

In my interaction with staff and students at different levels in our education system, I stress the importance and value of cocurricular activities, and how they facilitate the holistic development of students and impact their personal, professional, and leadership development.

I brought to The Mico the negotiating skills I developed as the head boy at Dinthill, which were further honed at the college.

In my time as a student at The Mico, there were just a few ladies who were enrolled as part of the student body. In order to balance the gender equity in our social interactions, we young men had to collaborate with Shortwood Teachers' College, which was an all-female college.

We would sometimes also partner with the all-female Nurses' Hostels, under management, respectively, by the Kingston Public Hospital (KPH) and the University Hospital of the West Indies (UHWI).

One of the staple and much anticipated social events in my time as a student was The Mico Party. The ladies from Shortwood were invited to be our guests and join us gentlemen, and the few other ladies of The Mico, in Classroom B or the Pavilion for a great time!

As first-year students (freshmen), it was our turn to invite our first-year counterparts from Shortwood Teachers' College.

All the ladies in this group were very attractive to the envy of the second-year men (senior men) at The Mico, who watched the ladies from the balcony of the Buxton Building as they took their leisurely walk to our party at the Pavilion.

After our party on a memorable Saturday night, three of us gentlemen—Astley Smith (who later became an outstanding dentist in Canada and Jamaica's honorary consul in Vancouver), George Binns (who became a brilliant educator in Toronto), and me—returned to the dormitory in the wee, very, very late "forbidden Mico hour" of 11:00 p.m.!

On our arrival, a group of second-year men met us at the top of the stairs in the Buxton Building, which housed the dormitory, with the ominous greeting, "Swing the grubs!"—i.e., "Report these freshmen to the principal!"

So said, so done.

Come Monday morning, my two sorry-looking batch mates and I, handcuffed by our guilt and grim with foreboding, were marched like criminals to the chambers of the principal/judge.

This all seemed like a case of déjà vu. I had been this way before.

Indeed I had already experienced the present situation, the precedence being the "case" involving an accused student at Dinthill. As head boy of the school, I took it upon myself to serve as counsel for the defense. The argument I had put forward in defense of the student ("remain in school on probation rather than expulsion") was so compelling that the principal/judge ruled in his favour, and I won the case!

I felt certain that as a more mature and experienced college man, I could repeat the feat.

It was, as is usually the case in these matters, an "in camera" hearing in the chambers/office of the principal/judge.

So it was with confidence, rather than trepidation, that I stepped forward, with cadet-drilled posture, and approached the "bench." In my best Wycliffe Bennett-coached diction, I presented my argument on behalf of all of us—the three co-accused.

"Sir, after the party was over, as the good Mico men you have taught us to be, we escorted the ladies from Shortwood to the bus stop at Cross Roads and waited until they were safely on the bus before we returned to college, albeit late."

The principal/judge, Mr. Glen Owen, without objection, replied, "Very good, gentlemen."

There was nothing more to be said by either party.

And just like that, the case was dismissed. Case closed!

My co-accused and I walked out of "court' as light as air. Freed of the dread of an uncertain outcome and the burden of what-if speculations, we were as pleased and proud of ourselves as we could ever be.

Of course the second-year men were furious when they heard that there would be no charges against us. They were so incensed that there was even a suggestion that they would take the law into their own hands and deliver suitable punishment of their own choosing.

But I was well protected from their vitriol, and their threats, because I had the privilege and good fortune of being one of eight first-year students who shared space with a group of third-year students in the dormitory under the Buxton Tower.

Now this group of third-year students included highly ranked and esteemed personages, including Headley Simms, president of the Student Council; Winston "Rabbi" Wright; Leo Oates; Bruce Johnson; Roy Shaw; Lloyd Whinstanley; Sammy Myers; and Horace Lewis.

They all became my lifelong friends. Horace Lewis and I, in later years, went on to work together as colleague lecturers in physical education and sports at The Mico. My relationship with these gentlemen was then, and continues to be, very special.

Horace reminded me recently that I was the freshman with the big voice, who was affectionately regarded by them as a "squatter" in the third-year dormitory. Now, I am a squatter no more in their regard for me, as they have adopted me as a member of their graduating class, the 59ers.

When you are in college, there are indeed endless opportunities to interact with a diverse range of people, at all levels, on and off campus. These interactions provide excellent opportunities for honing networking skills, which are so vital to effective leadership.

In those days, although morals were not an official subject about which you sat for an examination, you could nonetheless fail the subject.

Glen Owen, who was then principal of The Mico, declared that a requirement for graduation was to become a member of a church.

It was therefore important for a student to do so.

One student, in seeking to comply with the edict, went to get baptized at a church in downtown Kingston. After his third quick immersion, his feet, somewhat miraculously (or accursedly, depending on one's perspective), rose above the water for all to see.

His socks, or what was left of them, had great big holes in them! This vision created a not quite successful, muted stir among the gathering. It was later, after the ceremony, however, that the "holey visitation" was subject to much loud and unbridled outbursts of laughter! Poor fellow.

My effort at compliance with the church membership order was not as spectacular.

I became a member of St. Matthew's Anglican Church in Allman Town, and a member of the Brotherhood of St. Andrew, neither of which involved immersion in water, nor were my socks or other garments holey, though poor in quality they may have been.

My batch of male students was the last to live in the Buxton Building and the first set of men to live in the newly opened Mills Hall. My two other partners in crime from the infamous "Late Arrival to Campus Case" became my roommates. One went on to be elected president of the Student Guild, the other became president of the graduating class, and I became secretary of the Student Guild. Three powerful Mico men who "run tings" were together in one room. Mercy!

One year, during our tenure as student leaders, a ship that had docked in the Kingston Harbour invited students of The Mico to visit the ship.

Twelve tickets were allotted to the leadership of the Student Guild to distribute as they wished among the student body.

We three "wise men" determined that it was only right that the three of us should avail ourselves of two tickets each to accommodate our girlfriends, whom we would invite to accompany us. We thought it fair that the remaining six tickets be raffled off among the wider student body.

We were very open and transparent with the students about the decision-making process and the rationale for same.

One vociferous member of our opposition, Sexton, was quite disturbed and upset about the entire affair. He eventually relented, however, and went along with the decision on the basis that at least we were "open and honest."

In hindsight, that leadership decision was not one of my proudest moments.

Back then, however, as a trio of student leaders and good friends, we were more wise *guys* than wise *men*.

From the experience, I learnt two very important leadership lessons.

Leadership Lessons

Lesson 1: *Be authentic.* It is of vital importance to let others, especially those whom you lead, know where you stand on issues. Dealing straightforwardly with others is the key to authentic leadership.

Lesson 2: *Be open and honest.* This is important at all times, and especially when there may be times when your leadership decision is unpopular and out of favour with those whom you lead and serve.

Even though Sexton thought we were being self-serving, with respect to the ticket distribution, he eventually quieted down and acceded to the decision, based only on the transparency and honesty that attended our handling of the matter.

Truly, when all else fails, the truth will set you free.

As a student of The Mico, I started learning about strategic thinking, strategic planning, and strategic action. As I learnt more about the subjects, I began to reflect on my knowledge of and experience with the dance hall, and I began to see certain parallels.

Upon closer examination I thought to myself, what better place to experience and/or demonstrate strategic thinking, planning, and action than in the dance hall!

Let's dance!

During the holidays, I would attend Sound System Dance sessions at places like Springfield Club and The Roof in my hometown, Morant Bay.

The Roof, as the name suggests, was actually the roof of a building that housed a jewelry store, a restaurant, and a bar. It was a concrete slab roof, which was converted into a patio, complete with iron rails around its perimeter. It was the spot that you went to on a Wednesday evening to enjoy easy-listening music and romantic songs.

Some nights The Roof was the place for exciting domino competitions. Dance sessions were on Friday evenings.

Springfield Club was the clubhouse for the St. Thomas Cricket Team and was about five miles from the center of the town, across the road from the old Goodyear Tyre Factory.

This clubhouse consisted of the cricket club's offices and a fair-sized rectangular space for meetings, as well as where the cricket teams had lunch and refreshments during a cricket match.

This was also the area where dance sessions were held and at which one of the three sound systems in Morant Bay played on a Saturday night, or had a "clash" involving all three of them. It was the dance hall spot to be at on a Saturday night.

In that era, the dance hall at The Roof or Springfield Club had some important structures and processes one must understand in order to negotiate one's way effectively through the session—and have a great time.

First, the dance floor was informally organized in three sections. Young persons would dance at the front section. When you became a little older, you danced in the middle section. The back section was reserved for the "big people dem, who carry on big people things!"

My friends, including David Telfer, Basil McCalla, and Richard Phidd, and I "graduated" over time, from the front section when we were in high school to the middle section by the time David and I became college men at The Mico, and Richard and Basil had moved up to the Upper Sixth Form at Excelsior High School.

Whichever section you were in, however, you had to think and plan for "lockdown time." This was the time when the mood of the music would change, and you and your desired partner (if you planned well) would be engaged in a smooth and sensuous, hip-grinding "rent a tile," i.e., the art of dancing in place and in rhythm on only one small square of space.

You would be considered "very salt," i.e., out of it, if when lockdown time came, you had not yet secured the attention and interest of that special girl to dance with. In such an instance, the nice, "soff" (soft) soul music would be considered wasted if your preferred dance partner was not with you.

To ensure that such a fate does not befall you, there are a few tried and proven strategic moves that you must make.

Number 1—From early on in the evening, you have to start engaging the young lady you have eyes on in serious conversation, generously laced with good lyrics.

During such a softening-up/getting-to-know-you encounter, be confident and articulate, without being "nuff"/cocky and overbearing. To do otherwise is to risk coming across to the young lady as boorish, nerdy, or conceited—none of which will get you to lockdown with her on the dance floor.

Ensure too that you are a good listener. Give the young lady a chance to breathe and hear herself think, without constantly yapping in her ears so she can hardly get a word in edgewise. Let her speak; be interested in what she has to say. Manage the conversation in such a way that the young lady is interested, engaged, and is an active participant in the conversation. Before you know it, you could be waltzing her into lockdown.

Number 2—Amid the conversation with "your" young lady, be mindful of the flow and rhythm of the music. Follow the selector/DJ keenly to ensure that you are on the dance floor with your partner for the last two tunes before the lockdown music starts.

To be so strategically positioned is to ensure that when the lockdown selections begin, you and your partner are ready to go with the flow of the music and the "energy" between you, and just "lock eeen" (lock in) and hold tight to the groove.

If you follow this two-step strategy as smoothly as the two-step dance move, not only will you have achieved lockdown status with your young lady during lockdown time, but you also may further succeed in making a move or two with her, beyond the dance floor.

Believe me, I know of what I speak as an experienced dance hall aficionado, and as one who is the former executive director of the Mona School of Business at the University of the West Indies, Mona Campus. There is a great deal of value in the study and application of dance-hall strategies to strategic thinking, planning, and action.

You may well find that the steps to take to secure timely lockdown of your strategic goals may well be facilitated and enabled more by the experience and utilization of dance-hall strategies than any business school training ever could. Trust me.

The underlying lesson in this story is one that is shared several times throughout this book, but it bears repeating for emphasis.

Leadership Lesson

Leadership skills and competencies can be acquired and/or developed through conventional, formal educational settings, as well as informally in nonconventional settings. The bottom line is that all of life experiences are lessons in leadership…if we are alert to them!

I think at this stage of my life, as part of my continuing education and lifelong learning approach to life and living, I need to become an active participant in the now more modern and contemporary dance hall sessions, and explore and discover the new lessons to be learnt and applied to strengthen and deepen my leadership capacity.

Methinks it could be a strategic move.

In my hometown, Morant Bay, there was a Mr. Wynter, an older gentleman, who was the manager of the appliance store in the town. His marketing strategy for selling his sound equipment was to play a range of musical selections from different genre, including jazz, R and B, and classical music.

He would play a rich and varied mix of music, such as "Smoke Gets in Your Eyes" by the Platters, "Take Five" by the Dave Brubeck Quartet, "All Shook Up" by Elvis Presley, "Rock Around the Clock" by Bill Haley and the Comets, "The Blue Danube" waltz, "Cherry Pink and Apple Blossom White" by Perez Prado; "Chances Are" by Johnny Mathis, "Puppy Love" by Paul Anka, and classical compositions from Bach, Beethoven, Mozart, Stravinsky, Handel, Bizet, and Verdi…among other genres.

Mr. Wynter's public broadcast of music prepared me well for the music lessons we had with Olive Lewin. She would often give us an assignment to listen to the radio broadcast "Classical Music Hour" aired on RJR every Sunday afternoon.

The following Monday morning, when classes resumed, we would present a report on what we had heard and how what we heard made us feel.

I thoroughly enjoyed and fully appreciated the value of these music appreciation lessons, particularly the immersion in classical music appreciation.

Many years later, after listening to stories of The Mico, as recounted in lively conversation between her husband, Professor Edwin Jones, and me, Maria Jones, a distinguished executive management professional in both the public and private sector, remarked, "Now I know where my husband developed his love and appreciation for classical music!"

Edwin was my junior at The Mico. He was an outstanding athlete (a sprinter) and a brilliant student. These accomplishments did not prevent him, however, from getting up to some mischief from time to time.

One such time was when, with a near disastrous consequence, he focused his dubious attention and interest on my friend David Telfer, whom, it is significant to note, was also senior to him.

David had by now developed quite a pronounced and hefty paunch. Edwin's discerning eye quickly took in the span of David's girth, and his brilliant mind declared him to be Santa Claus!

Now, had Edwin noted his discernment in silence and kept the thought to himself, without need of public declaration, all would have been well. But no, he didn't. It would have been prudent to do, but prudence is not always a factor when one is up to mischief.

So one day, with no pretense of affection and with mild derision, he hailed David as "Santa Claus!" and all hell and the "North Pole" broke loose! Rudolph and all the other reindeer and the elves scattered, as

Edwin had to dive through the window in Classroom B to escape David's wrath.

This memorable event resulted in the beginning of lifelong friendship between Edwin and his batch mates, Ayton Taylor and C. K. Robinson, who were also members of the Dinthill clan. They became Edwin's "security team."

Edwin was also adopted as a member of the Wise Men from the East Club. This club consisted of students from St. Thomas and Portland who attended Dinthill and then The Mico. Its members included C. K. Robinson, Lloyd Stanley, David Telfer, and me from St. Thomas, and Albert Neufville, Ken Neysmith, and Ralph Kirkland from Portland.

I am happy to say that after graduating from The Mico, Edwin and I caught up with each other as students in the hallowed halls of academia at the UWI. We later served together in advancing the vision and mission of the UWI.

Edwin became a distinguished professor and the dean of the faculty of social sciences.

I undertook the pioneering task of establishing the first EMBA (Executive Masters in Business Administration) programme at UWI and laying the foundation for the Mona Institute of Business, which later evolved into the Mona School of Business (now renamed Mona School of Business and Management). Edwin played a pivotal role in assisting me with these initiatives.

When I served as executive director of the Mona School of Business, Edwin also assisted me greatly in developing the doctorate in business administration (DBA), and the joint Mico/Mona School of Business (MSB) master's programme in education and business management.

Through my experience with Edwin, whom I met in college and

became lifelong friends with, I learnt, as I did through all my other friends, an essential lesson:

Solid friendships formed earlier in life can play a significant role later in life to facilitate success of your leadership initiatives.

The Mico, as with all college experiences, is home to countless opportunities, both personal and professional.

From the day I set foot on The Mico campus, I knew I had walked into a gold mine of possibilities. Just meeting the wide variety of individuals, all with their own strengths, goals, dreams, and circles of influence, was treasure enough.

The basic underpinning of networking, a skill that is so crucial to effective leadership, is the recognition that each person has something of value to offer.

The lesson for leaders is to learn how to, as the Center for Creative Leadership, USA, puts it, "develop and utilize networks in such a way as to build relationships and strengthen alliances in service of your organization's work and goals."

Another important lesson I learnt at The Mico is this:

Be careful about how "the halo effect" impacts your judgement as a leader.

Kendra Cherry, author, psychosocial rehabilitation specialist, and educator, provides a very good summary understanding of the "halo effect" in her article: "Why the Halo Effect Influences How we perceive others", reviewed by Amy Morin, July 19, 2020 :

"The halo effect is a type of <u>cognitive bias</u> in which our overall impression of a person influences how we feel and think about their character. Essentially, your overall impression of a person ("he is nice")impacts your evaluations of that person's specific traits ("he is also smart". Perceptions of a single trait can carry over to how we perceive other aspects of that person."

The following stories will illustrate this point.

My roommate Astley really believed in a good and healthy mix of fun and study. On any evening, we would go to see a movie at the Carib Theatre in Cross Roads, then return to campus to study.

One night we returned late, about 9:30 p.m., and went directly to the study room in Mills Hall. The other students who had been studying since 7:00 p.m. had all left for bed.

Mr. McMillian, one of our lecturers, was doing his nightly round of checks and saw only the two of us in the study room.

The next day, in his class, he lauded us, and held us up before our peers, as exemplars of diligence and discipline, saying to the class that they "should all try to be studious like Ying and Smith."

Astley and I also consistently earned top marks, between A and B, as our grade for the course that he taught. They were well-deserved grades, but I do believe we may have earned a point or two extra because of his perception of our diligence and commitment to study.

Most weekends Astley and I would go off to Mandeville to spend the weekend with his older brother, who worked there. We would attend whatever party or fun social event was happening there.

Now here's the rub: each Monday, we were required to hand in an essay for one of our classes, which we were all expected to do over the weekend.

Astley and I, knowing that our weekend was spent in social pursuits, would, on the said Monday, use the midmorning hour during "Pug" (refreshment break) to write our respective essays.

We scored no less than A or B, and the same range of grades in the final examination.

The halo effect could have led to the conclusion that we would be failures in our studies, as we spent too much time gallivanting when we should be studying and doing our assignments.

Religious education was not my forte, so I would study the week before the examination with people such as Clifton Lawrence and Ronnie Walters (who became a minister of religion after graduation).

They were both very knowledgeable students, experts even, in this subject. Somehow, their influence and input and my own marginal efforts in the study of the subject resulted in me earning equally high marks as they did in the examinations.

The lecturer in this subject thought that I was a "bright" religious education student. This perception was solidified in his mind when he thought my answer to a question on the Lord's Prayer (having not done any prior study and analysis of it), was a "model answer of excellence."

He was however surprised at my high level of performance because his presumption was that because I was a mathematics and physics major, I had no serious interest in religious education, and therefore I would not do as well as I did in the subject.

Equally, because he considered Clifton and Ronnie as students who were quite interested in and adept at the subject, he expected that they would excel and perform heads and shoulders above everyone else.

Again the Halo Effect in operation.

At The Mico, I also began to learn more about business.

My two roommates and I decided to propose a business venture to our graduating class at The Mico and our counterpart graduating class from Shortwood. The proposal was that we would stage our own Graduation Ball as an entrepreneurial venture. We offered shares to investors.

Only a few persons—other than us, the initiators—took up the offer and invested. It was therefore a big risk to continue with the venture as proposed, given the paucity of funds and, in the initial stages, lack of interest by potential patrons.

We, the bold and intrepid entrepreneurs, went ahead with the plans, regardless.

As luck would have it, the band we engaged for the event, Byron Lee and the Dragonaires, was just at the beginning stage of its musical career. They were very popular, but at that stage of their journey, they welcomed any and every platform to perform in order to further establish themselves as an outstanding band on the entertainment scene.

We were also fortunate to secure the use of the Myrtle Bank Hotel as the for our Graduation Ball.. This stately, world-famous hotel of longstanding was akin in prestige and status to the Jamaica Pegasus Hotel of today. It was located on Harbour Street in Kingston which now houses the Grace Kennedy Car Park and the Jamaica Stock Exchange Building, which maintains the original architecture of an annex to the old Myrtle Bank Hotel.

It is interesting to note that years later, when I worked in the private sector as a corporate vice president of the ICD Group of companies, my office was at its head office on Harbour Street, close to where the Myrtle Bank Hotel was located.

Even more interesting is that I currently chair two of the committees of the Jamaica Stock Exchange, and therefore, technically, I am a regular visitor to the former Annex of the Myrtle Bank Hotel, which once long ago, in the inglorious racist and elitist past, was a forbidden social space for dark-skinned persons like me.

But back to the venture of the Graduation Ball…

The event was a huge social and financial success. Those of us who had invested gained some much-needed start-up cash with which to begin our teaching careers after graduation.

That entire experience, from bold start to successful finish, was yet another invaluable precursor to and preparation for my life of service leadership in general, and business specifically.

In closing this chapter, I am exceedingly grateful that my college experience was rooted in The Mico's rich, diverse, student-centered and leadership-focused teaching and learning environment.

The Mico does indeed honour its promise and its claim to provide students with opportunities for "academic success, professional advancement, and the development of a solid transformational leadership character."

Quality leadership, as illustrated by the stories I have shared, isn't a cut-and-dried quality however. It is quite nuanced. There are so many component parts, each requiring their own unique set of skills to be effective.

The multiple responsibilities of managing and maintaining a

demanding programme of study and cocurricular activities, dealing with social and personal obligations, and performing leadership roles effectively combined to provide excellent opportunities to hone many of the skills I required to face and overcome the personal, social, and professional challenges of the "real world."

The experiences at the collegiate level, through The Mico, has had a profound impact in shaping the quality of my leadership and my capacity to successfully negotiate my way through life's maze of challenges, even as I am charged to simultaneously lead and guide others through.

I am grateful to The Mico for its commitment to leadership as a vital component of the educational experience by "developing and nurturing ethical and value-based individuals who will exert positive influence and be agents of transformative changes in whatever institution and community they serve."

I am especially grateful that The Mico's core values and mine were mutually aligned. It is those core values that have solidified my servant leadership.

I am as committed as The Mico is "to the practice of service for the well-being and improved quality of life of others through habits of empathy, caring, empowerment, and civic and social responsibility."

It is said that leadership is about the art of motivating, influencing, and directing people.

I add to that…

Servant Leadership Philosophy

Helping others to achieve their true potential is your most important mission in life.

6

Advancing the Servant Leader:
Stories, Lessons, and Impact of University and Continued Higher Learning

> Some learning processes will undoubtedly challenge you...
> and even be a source of discomfort at times.
> Embrace the process and learn as much as you can
> remembering that you are being prepared
> for a purpose greater than yourself.
> Leadership qualities are being developed in you.
> —Unknown

THE MICO, THE first higher education institution I attended, had prepared me well for the next steps in my higher education journey.

The holistic education and learning environment that The Mico provided enabled me to become optimally rounded—academically socially, morally, physically, and spiritually—and to be strengthened in the learning and development of valuable life and leadership skills.

Graduating from The Mico opened the gateway to a successful teaching career at Denham Town School and St. Andrew Technical High

School and beyond. Despite this situation I did an assessment of my future career path.

Based on this assessment I was led to the decision that my upward mobility in the management structure of an educational institution required having a degree, in addition to my teacher education diploma.

I decided, therefore, that it would be both personally and professionally strategic and satisfying if I enrolled in further studies at a university. This would also serve to strengthen my commitment to lifelong learning,

As such, I applied and gained acceptance to Cornell University in the USA. My economic circumstances, however, would not allow me to take up the offer. I simply had no money.

My former batch mate at The Mico and good friend, Rupert Burey, knowing of my desire to attend university, shared with me information he gleaned from someone he knew, who worked at the Ministry of Education. His informant told him that teachers' scholarships in mathematics and science were available for the University of the West Indies (UWI).

Rupert, Eric Bramwell, Claude Evans, and I, who were all mathematics specialists and batch mates at The Mico, applied and successfully sat for the scholarship examination to gain entry to the UWI as recipients of teachers' scholarships.

I took with me to UWI the deeply ingrained principle that is at the heart of The Mico ethos, and that encourage students to...

> take responsibility for their learning, to strive for excellence in their studies and conduct, to fully participate in and be meaningfully involved in academic, non-academic, and service activities, and to take full advantage of the opportunities for career and personal development.

The University of the West Indies (UWI)

The University of the West Indies (UWI) boasts a rich and enduring history. It was originally instituted as an independent external College of the University of London—University College of the West Indies (UCWI).

The UWI is now a public university system established to serve the higher education needs of the residents of seventeen English-speaking countries and territories in the Caribbean: Anguilla, Antigua and Barbuda, the Bahamas, Barbados, Belize, Bermuda, British Virgin Islands, Cayman Islands, Dominica, Grenada, Jamaica, Montserrat, St. Kitts and Nevis, St. Lucia, St. Vincent and the Grenadines, Trinidad and Tobago, and Turks and Caicos Islands.

The UWI's vision is to "be globally recognized as a regionally integrated, innovative, internationally competitive university, deeply rooted in all aspects of Caribbean development and committed to serving the diverse people of the region and beyond."

The UWI's mission is "to advance education and create knowledge through excellence in teaching, research, innovation, public service, intellectual leadership and outreach in order to support the inclusive (social, economic, political, cultural, environmental) development of the Caribbean region and beyond."

The core values that guide the institution's mandate, policy, and decision-making are integrity, intellectual freedom, excellence, civic responsibility, accessibility, diversity, and equity.

One of the main strategic aims of the UWI is "to unlock the potential for economic and cultural growth in the West Indies" through the development of "a cadre of individuals who will be able to tackle the many existing as well as emerging government, business and societal related challenges and, proffer the relevant innovative solutions."

The institution operates from major university centres: UWI Mona (Jamaica), UWI Cave Hill (Barbados), UWI St. Augustine (Trinidad and Tobago), the regional UWI Open Campus, and more recently the UWI Five Islands Campus (Antigua).

The UWI over the years has made significant contributions to prepare individuals for leadership at both the organizational and national levels.

The UWI's undergraduate, master's and doctoral students, as well as its faculty, came from all parts of Jamaica, other Caribbean countries, and around the world. Thus, the institution has a strong multidimensional character.

Through the years, the UWI has produced students who have excelled in and provided leadership in a number of disciplines—the arts, sciences, business, research and development, political science, management, communication, international relations, and others—and who have served in key leadership positions in the region and around the world.

One poignant example of this is the area of political leadership.

Developing and nurturing students' interest and consciousness in political leadership aspirations, in their respective Caribbean states, was of vital importance to the UWI.

Some of the UWI graduates who are, or have been, heads of government, in their respective counties are as follows:

Jamaica—Andrew Holness, current prime minister; P. J. Patterson, former prime minister; Bruce Golding, former prime minister

Trinidad and Tobago—Keith Rowley, current prime minister; Kamla Persad-Bissessar, first female prime minister; Patrick Manning, former prime minister

Barbados—Freundel Stuart, former prime minister; Lloyd Erskine Sandiford, former prime minister; David Thompson, former prime minister; Owen Arthur, former prime minister

St. Kitts and Nevis—Timothy Harris, current prime minister; Vance Amory, former premier; Denzil Douglas, former prime minister; Kennedy A. Simmonds, former prime minister; Joseph Walcott Parry, former premier of Nevis

St. Lucia—Kenny Anthony, former prime minister

Belize—Dean Barrow, prime minister

Turks and Caicos Islands—Rufus Ewing, current premier

St. Vincent and the Grenadines—Ralph Gonsalves, current prime minister

Guyana—David A. Granger, president of Guyana

Bahamas—Hubert Minnis, prime minister

Grenada—Keith Mitchell, current prime minister; Tillman Thomas, former prime minister

British Virgin Islands—Orlando Smith, chief minister

The Students' Guild and Halls of Residences provided excellent preparation and platforms from which to launch the political leadership ambitions and fulfillment of many students who went on to serve as candidates in their respective national elections.

The UWI's vision, mission, strategic intentions, core values, and track record in the area of leadership development provided me with an environment conducive to further shaping me as a servant leader.

In my era, involvement in academic pursuits and cocurricular activities was facilitated by the structure of our programme of studies and related examinations.

We did examinations for Part 1 of the degree programme at the end of our first year, and we then did examinations for part 2 of the degree programme, at the end of our third year.

This kind of schedule meant that the second year of the degree programme offered great opportunities to participate more fulsomely in clubs; societies; sports—cricket, soccer, hockey, lawn tennis, track and field, badminton, and hockey; plus a wide range of musical performances.

As a student at the UWI, Mona Campus, from impressive start to glorious finish, it positively impacted my servant leadership development.

There were many important leadership lessons learnt and leadership skills developed that enabled me to become an effective servant leader. I will now share these with you.

Servant Leadership Lesson

It is important to listen to and accommodate radically different ideas and viewpoints.

The opportunity for learning this lesson was that in my time as a student at the UWI, Mona Campus, my fellow students included persons who went on to hold high political office or impact the affairs of politics and governance in the Caribbean.

Some of these persons are as follows:

Ralph Gonsalves—current and longest-serving (since 2001) prime minister of St. Vincent and the Grenadines

The late Hon. Patrick Manning—former fourth prime minister of Trinidad and Tobago

Hon. Robert Pickersgill—former minister of government, Jamaica

Hon Johnny Cheltenham—former minister of government, Barbados

Professor/Hon. Carl Stone, OM—political sociologist who pioneered the systematic study of voting behaviour in Jamaica

Professor Trevor Munroe—political scientist, Civil Society advocate and current executive director of National Integrity Action (NIA), Jamaica.

Richard Jacobs, political scientist and Grenada's Ambassador to Russia.

These were certainly exciting times while I was a UWI student. Expressing contending viewpoints and radically different ideas was an integral part of the interaction among students in my time. Organizing and staging protests about one thing or another was also a regular feature of the campus's sociopolitical landscape.

I recall with wry amusement an encounter I had with a passionate "protester," who was one of my hall mates and a social science student. I met him while I was on my way from the physics lab to our Hall of Residence.

He was shouting stridently, "Strike! Strike! Strike!"

I enquired of him what the issue was that he was protesting about. I was dumbstruck by his response.

"I don't know, but strike! Strike! Strike!"

Servant Leadership Lesson

It is important to live and work harmoniously with persons from different cultures while preserving your unique identity.

This leadership development environment was enriched by the diversity of students from CARICOM countries.

The experience of living on campus in a residence hall and attending classes with this diversity of fellow students provided me with the opportunity to learn about different cultures and living harmoniously with others, in spite of the differences.

Even more importantly, the experience enabled me to develop a consciousness about the importance of displaying a common *Caribbean citizen* profile, while maintaining my unique national identity

In this process I also started to learn in a practical way an important leadership skill: *diversity management (DM).*

DM is a strategic institutional and organizational commitment and approach, supported by programmes, activities, and mechanism, directed toward the integration and development of diversity and inclusivity.

DM promotes and provides opportunities for the full participation of everyone in institutional/organizational activities. It supports the individual characteristics of each and utilizes their unique characteristics as a strategic lever.

The overarching idea behind DM in institutions, therefore, is to ensure acknowledgment and acceptance of differences between and among the institutional community. In other words, *despite our differences, we all have to learn to live in peace and harmony.*

Leadership Impact of Cultural Activities and Sports

- **Impact of Cultural Activities**

The leadership impact of cultural activities and sports cannot be overlooked. There are many key servant leadership lessons to be learnt.

- **Servant Leadership Lesson**

Cultural activities and sports are important influencers in your development and functioning as a servant leader.

The following is a chronology of events that impacted my leadership development and preparation for future leadership roles in culture and entertainment.

- **Impact of Culture**

The UWI had a wide variety of cultural activities that impacted my leadership development.

It was at UWI that I was first exposed to the Carnival of Trinidad and Tobago. The carnival was celebrated annually in the twin-island state and in other Eastern Caribbean Islands, but it was imported by the students from those islands into Jamaica, which did not then have a "carnival culture."

In those days in Jamaica, the carnival was confined only to the UWI, Mona Campus—unlike now, when the Jamaica Carnival is enjoyed by a wide cross section of persons across Jamaica.

Back then at the UWI, during carnival season, there were numerous cultural events, such as the Calypso Competition, Carnival Queen Show, Carnival Road March on the "Ring Road"...and of course, J'ouvert.

One year, I was a member of the composing and production team in Taylor Hall ,Block E, working on our bold entry in the Carnival Song Competition.

Those of us from Jamaica—George Campbell, Ronnie Young, and I—wrote the lyrics, and Kemal Ali, a student from T&T, composed the music and performed the song, accompanied by George Campbell, an exceptional guitarist from Jamaica.

We had high expectations of winning the competition. Regrettably, the outcome was not what we had expected. We found out later, however, that the main reason we did not win was that the ladies from the all-female Mary Seacole Hall were rather put out (annoyed) with our lyrics.

That year, Mary Seacole Hall won the Carnival Costume Competition, with all due credit to the outstanding artistic talent of Gillian Bishop from T&T (Trinidad and Tobago).

Then there was J'ouvert, a highly anticipated predawn revelry.

Revelers, not costumed but all splashed or smeared with paint, would jump and dance in wild abandon to a noisy cacophony of shouts and music—aided and abetted, it must be admitted, by a "little" rum but mainly fueled by the exhilaration of the moment.

Irvine Hall was the leader in J'ouvert. One year, Rupert Burey, my batch mate from The Mico and my UWI mathematics and physics classmate, played the part of Caveman in the J'ouvert.

The organizers of the J'ouvert told him he did not need any special costume and that he should just appear, without combing his hair, and he would look perfect for the part. We both still laugh when we recall that particular story.

Our chemistry lecturer, no less a personage than the great Professor Gerald Lalor, was to our young and carnival-infused minds a real party-pooper, a veritable spoilsport.

Each year, at the fever-pitch height of the bacchanal—when the energy was at its peak, and the brain dulled by the potent fusion of music and dance—he would set a chemistry test for the Saturday morning following the Friday night's Carnival Queen Show.

Thanks to the powerful antidote of several cups of strong coffee, we survived and bested both the chemistry test and the "test" of our ability to effectively balance work and play.

I had the privilege of being a fellow student with the larger-than-life personality Maud Fuller—teacher, actor, dramatist, artistic director, and of theatre (Jamaica Pantomime) fame.

I was part of the team that worked with her on the production of *We Kiss in the Shadows*.

I will digress a little at this point to share with you that some scenes in this play reminded me of couples "trawlin'" (strolling) from the Halls of Residence to the plains—what is now the Mona Sports Bowl. In our time, you could win a guild election if you had in your manifesto, "Keeping the route from the Halls of Residence to the plains dark."

Back to the play...

I still remember the beautiful singing by Rowena Ahee (soprano) and Michael Phillips (tenor). They were both students from T&T. Michael was my fellow Taylorite (Taylor Hall) from Block D, and Rowena was from Mary Seacole Hall.

By then the rift (arising from our carnival song episode) between our two halls (Taylor Hall and Mary Seacole Hall) had ended.

This "mending of the breach" between the two halls was due in large measure to Ronnie and Willard from Taylor Hall, who formed romantic alliances with Pansy Williams and Georgia Lawrence from Mary Seacole Hall—whom they later married respectively.

One memorable incident during the play was when my friend and hall mate Harry, from T&T, forgot his lines, and Maud was cursing some choice words backstage. Her rant was interrupted, however, by the applause from the audience. From then on, Harry's new "improvised" lines were written into the script for subsequent performances.

The next dramatic production in which I was engaged was Shakespeare's *Macbeth*.

"If it were done when 'tis done, then 'twere well it were done quickly."

The production was staged outdoors at the Mona Visitors Lodge, in the vicinity of what is now the upgraded Ruins.

I played the lead role of Macbeth, supported by a brilliant cast of actors, including Keith Noel from Irvine Hall, Pauline Powell from Mary Seacole Hall, and Trevor Fitzhenley from Chancellor Hall.

Then there was the University Singers, begun in 1957, comprising UWI undergraduate and graduate students. It has distinguished itself as one of the leading choral groups in the Caribbean, widely noted for its versatility, spanning varied musical genres.

One of my classmates, the late Noel Dexter, OD, a distinguished musician and composer, was the musical director of the choir for thirty-three years.

Together with the late professor and former UWI vice chancellor, the

Honourable Rex Nettleford, as the artistic director, they developed what is widely acclaimed as an "avant-garde approach, referred to as choral theatre," which the group used to good performance effect and has boosted its standing tremendously.

Another of my classmates who was involved with the University Singers was Lilieth Nelson. She was a member of the choir from 1964 and became the musical director from 1971 to 1977 (Noel Dexter succeeded her). To her further credit, Lilieth started the Irvine Hall Choir, the first hall to have such a group. In later years, Lilieth received national honours for her "outstanding contribution to Jamaican culture."

My fellow Taylorite and friend from Grenada, "Pleck," who was also our barber, started teaching me to play the steel pan. This was fascinating stuff and so absorbing that I had to make a choice between learning to play the steel pan and physics lab work. Regrettably, physics won.

The other UWI Halls of Residence—Irvine, Mary Seacole, and Chancellor—had a great impact on me, particularly in the area of culture.

Irvine Hall, taking advantage of the rich diversity of its student population, conceptualized and successfully staged its annual flagship event, Culturama. This event earned the hall widespread respect, acclaim, and the distinction of being regarded as the "cultural mecca" of the UWI.

Culturama explores and expresses the different genres of Caribbean art and culture through a dynamic explosion and exposition of dancing, singing, fashion, and food.

Its main aim is to honour, celebrate, and educate its audience about the varying cultures in the Caribbean, highlighting something about each island's distinctive culture in an entertaining and appealing way.

Nuff respect to the Irvinites for their creativity!

Irvine was also famous for its "spine fetes." We men from Taylor Hall had great appreciation for the Irvinites for putting this on, as well as all of their other events.

The Irvinites had a song they sung when they won a football competition, which was a rare accomplishment. The same song (so little sung before) was sung with great gusto whenever they won—"We buss dey…!"

When they lost (which was often), the lyrics would be tweaked, and they would sing, rather forlornly (as they often did), "Dey buss we…"

Mary Seacole Hall and Chancellor Hall, not to be outdone in the culture arena, joined forces to stage the highly anticipated and enduring annual concert, Spectrum!

In my time, Spectrum was a concert that largely involved UWI students in performance, though these days, the lineup of performers includes non-UWI, well-established, and emerging wannabe stars.

Spectrum has continued to maintain its name and its fame throughout the years, and it has remained unchanged in its status of being a premier event on the UWI students' social calendar, as well as the halls' main and most profitable fundraising event.

In my time, however, student performers had to be careful about their performances because Chancellor Hall's warden, Dr. Bowen (Bo Bo), would, in his closing remarks, expose publicly seamy and/or steamy secrets of Chancellorite and Seacolite connections.

My involvement in these cultural and entertainment activities as an observer, as well as "actor," was important preparation ground for my leadership role in later years as a commissioner of the Jamaica Cultural Development Commission (JCDC).

Impact of Sports

In the area of sports, I had the honour, while I was a student at UWI, of serving as a line judge for badminton in the 1966 Commonwealth Games held in Jamaica.

This honour was due to the influence of Freddie Green, legendary footballer from Kingston College (KC) and outstanding sports lecturer and administrator.

He was my lecturer at The Mico when I specialized in physical education and sports, as well as mathematics and physics. He also knew that when I entered The Mico, I had already had competitive experience as a member of Dinthill's one-hundred-yard track team.

Based on this knowledge, Freddie Green recommended me to be a line judge for badminton at the Commonwealth Games. He also ensured that I was fully engaged in the rigorous training required prior to the games so I would perform that role effectively.

In my era as a student at UWI, there were no classes on Thursday afternoons, so on those afternoons I would play up to four hours of lawn tennis in the hot sun. I find it hard to believe that I could have undertaken what now seems to be such a monumental task, especially since these days I get tired just watching younger people playing tennis. *The joys of youth!*

My formal training in physical education and sports at The Mico, and my experiences as a volleyball coach at Denham Town School and assistant coach in track and field at St. Andrew Technical High School, together with my participation as an official in the 1966 Commonwealth Games while at UWI, served as great preparation to perform, in later years, key leadership roles in the arena of sports.

My first leadership role was as a sports administrator in the Intercollegiate Sports Association. In this sporting body, I served as vice president, alongside the president, Dr. Alfred Sangster.

When I succeeded Dr. Sangster as president, I served with sports stalwarts such as Dennis Johnson, Calabar High School fame and previous one-hundred-yards World Record holder; Vilma Charlton and Grace Jackson, Olympians; Edith Allen, The Mico; Claudette Jones, Church Teachers' College; Anthony Davis, former director of sports at the University of Technology (UTECH); and Edwin Murray, one of my former students from The Mico and former acting principal of G.C. Foster College.

I also benefitted tremendously from the experience and expertise of the late Teddy McCook, outstanding sports administrator and Kingston College "Old Boy."

These experiences proved to be of tremendous value to me in the area of policy formulation when I was asked by the prime minister and the minister of sports to perform the lead role in the preparation of the first National Sports Policy for Jamaica.

The value of my experiences in cultural activities and sports at UWI to my leadership roles after graduation reinforced one of the leadership lessons I learnt from my early childhood years.

Servant Leadership Lesson

Transfer of knowledge is an invaluable process in performing your servant leadership roles.

The Impact of Methodology for Learning and Succeeding on Leadership Development

- **Leadership Lesson**

Knowledge sharing and collaboration are important processes for effective servant leadership.

An important strategy that was used for performing well in our examinations was to form a study group from the first term when I entered UWI.

This group consisted of five of us who lived in Taylor Hall and pursued a programmer of studies in the faculty of natural sciences.

The modus operandi of this group was that each member would perform a leadership role for assignments and readings for a subject area.

The leadership roles were assigned as follows:

Paul Chance—physics, Willard Pinnock—chemistry, Claude Stewart—laboratory work for chemistry and physics, Ronnie Young—zoology, and me—mathematics.

Lilieth Nelson from Irvine Hall joined us and was the only female member of the group.

In recalling our study group, I realized how much I had learnt about Catholic schools, with respect to their approach to study. I learnt this because, as it turned out, three of the six members of our study group attended St. George's College (a Catholic high school).

The study routine they learnt at St. George's College and shared with us was that the secret of study success is to study three hours every night, and then a week before examinations, take a break, relax, and play cards or chess, or listen to music...whatever.

Our group fully embraced, and was committed to, this study routine. So, Ronnie, well-schooled in St. George's study method, had us all tuned in to this routine with music such as "The Girl from Ipanema." Though the actual girl from Ipanema was missing, the melody and the imagination truly relaxed us.

Many years later, when I did in fact visit the Ipanema Beach in Rio, Brazil, while attending the United Nations Conference on Sustainable Development, I found out that Ipanema was truly a haven for beautiful girls…though I daresay, back then, the girl from Ipanema was not only out of Ronnie's sight but also out of his reach!

Mark you, after dutifully studying for three hours each evening, we would then take a respite from study and head up to the nearby commercial district of Papine to have coffee.

I was amazed when Ronnie told me that after all these many long years, he saw the waiter who had served us our coffee in Papine. Quite remarkably, the said waiter remembered us! I guess we must have been memorable for more than just coffee stains.

After our coffee fix in Papine, we would then head to the campus's Students' Union to hang out with other students, almost all of whom clearly seemed to practice St. George's study method. These students included Trevor Munroe, who was a past student of St. George's College.

Trevor, incidentally, was quite resourceful in securing, even at short notice, the favour of young ladies as social partners. One such time was when one of the medical students in Taylor Hall arrived late from T&T on the day of the Freshmen's Ball.

Naturally, we called on our "trusty" Trevor to find him a young lady from Mary Seacole Hall to accompany him to the ball.

Not only was Trevor successful in the quest, and the freshman was able to enjoy the favour of a young lady on his arm at the ball, but also said freshman eventually graduated, and decided to reside in Jamaica.

Following our little respite at the Students' Union, which followed the Papine coffee fix, we Taylorites would then return to one of our rooms for an "ST" (small talk) session.

These sessions would revolve mostly around our favourite topic: *girls!*…especially those girls from the UHWI School of Nursing, more affectionately known as the "Bastille."

The background to this focus on the Bastille is that Irvine Hall was coed, and Chancellor Hall and Mary Seacole Hall formed an alliance.

So the men from Taylor Hall, facilitated by the large number of medical students who lived in the hall, formed an alliance with the young ladies from the UHWI School of Nursing, who resided in the compound of the UHWI Hospital, close to Taylor Hall.

Back to St. George's study method…

Truth is the St. George's study method worked! We were all successful students.

The irony of it all was that although we were widely perceived to be "time wasters," we never failed to pass our examinations…and with flying colors too! It was even more surprising to many that some of us went on to achieve higher levels of academic success, with some even becoming professors at UWI!

In later years, Lil has become even more special to us, due to her unwavering commitment to keeping all of us, as former members of the study group, in touch with each other through the years.

An amusing related story is that everyone in our study group was called by their surname. So Lil was known as Nelson. Years after graduation, whenever her name was mentioned in conversation with my wife, she assumed that this "Nelson" I referred to was a guy. This was cleared up many years later when my wife actually met Lil.

It is with deep sadness that I note, however, the passing of two of our study group members: Claude Stewart and Willard Pinnock, as well as Georgia Pinnock (nee Lawrence), Willard's wife.

The experiences from my study group at UWI proved to be invaluable to my servant leadership role in different organizations, during which I stress the importance of knowledge sharing and teamwork. I also stress the importance of these processes when I teach transformational leadership at UWI.

The Impact of Hall Life on Leadership Development

Hall life had a critical impact on leadership development and leadership skills.

- **Leadership Skill—Social Graces**

One of the skills that is of vital importance to everyone, and especially leaders, is social graces.

When the University College of the West Indies (UCWI) started classes in 1948, the "gown" (symbol of academia) was mandatory daily wear for students and lecturers, and for student dinner in the hall.

By the time I got to the UWI as a student, however, students were only required to wear their gowns to formal dinners in the hall, five nights each week.

These formal dinners were a great source of cultural experiences, from which I learnt two important lessons. The first was Social Graces.

One night per week, we were each to invite, as our guest, a young lady to dine with us. My friend Irene Walter (who later became, among other things, an esteemed educator and the first pro-registrar of CXC and later its registrar), was one such young lady who we invited to be a dinner guest.

Irene doubled as student and a member of staff of the UWI Registry. She successfully balanced work and study to join with me and other students as a member of our graduating class.

Before dinner, we had to formally meet and greet the ladies who were our guests, engage them in polite conversation, and offer them drinks, after which we would escort them to their table and assigned seating.

These formal dining occasions were designed to help students develop the various social graces associated with dining and etiquette, such as appropriate use of tableware, conversation, and the general exercise of good manners. These skills would prove to be beneficial in our personal and professional lives in later years.

Of course, as students, we had to create some pranks to enliven this rather stiff, though not exactly boring, occasion. Part of this "enlivening" process involved putting the salt, pepper, and salad dressing in front of one of the men sitting beside the young lady who was his guest.

During dinner, we would constantly ask him to pass one of those condiments to us and, with exaggerated politeness, return them to him.

This ongoing interruption would thereby enable the other gentleman sitting beside her to seize and optimize the opportunity for conversation…rich with the possibility for follow-up contact with her.

The second lesson was the importance of effective oral presentation.

- Leadership Skill—Effective Oral Presentations

Effective oral presentations incorporate the value and importance of making brief, succinct, informative, and engaging presentations as a leader.

At dinner, it was usual for various persons to be called upon, planned or spontaneously, to deliver a presentation on a certain topic.

Should the hapless presenter exceed five minutes in their presentation, the entire hall would shout in unison, "Finally!" This was the signal to stop talking because no one would be listening beyond that point.

A good example of a "brief" presentation involved Leon Welds from Grenada, who was elected as the hall librarian. He was also a student who worked as a server to earn extra money.

While he was coming from the kitchen, the men shouted, "Welds's library report!"

Welds put down the tray with the bowls of soup he was serving and began his presentation with the opening statement, "When I took over the library, it was in a mess."

At that point, the entire hall shouted spontaneously and in unison, "And it still is!"

That was the end of the Welds library report.

These two valuable leadership skills—social graces and effective oral presentations served me well in later years when I had to exhibit social engagement and effective presentations, especially when I represented Jamaica in international and regional fora.

University of Maryland (UM)

My travel to the University of Maryland (UM) was akin to taking the British West Indian Airways (BWIA) flight to Trinidad and Tobago.

In those days, the BWIA flight path would take you from Kingston to Montego Bay, Jamaica, and then on to stops in Port Au Prince, Haiti; San Juan, Puerto Rico; Antigua, Barbados; and finally, Trinidad and Tobago.

This journey was labelled the "milk run," referring to the days in Jamaica when a milk truck would collect fresh milk from dairy farmers at different points across the island and take it, finally, to the condensery for processing. Jokingly, BWIA was referred to as an acronym for "but will it arrive!"

Having graduated from UWI, I completed two successful working assignments, one at The Mico and the other at the Ministry of Education (MOE), Jamaica, before deciding that it was time to do postgraduate studies.

I had the amazing good fortune to be offered two scholarships for further academic studies at two overseas universities.

The first offer was a scholarship to attend Stanford University and pursue a master's degree in education. This offer was facilitated by the late Shirley Gordon, an outstanding educator who worked, at the time, as a consultant with Jamaica's Ministry of Education (MOE).

The second offer was a three-year, fully paid Government of Jamaica (civil service) scholarship for a programme of studies at a university of my choice.

I chose this second offer in the area of measurement, statistics, and research designs (the core areas of psychometrics) for my graduate studies, leading toward a doctoral degree.

My choice of academic programme was based on two considerations:

Consideration 1—Governments of CARICOM countries were engaged in serious discussion pursuant to a decision to replace the prevailing UK-based Cambridge and London Examination bodies in favour of the establishment of a new Caribbean Examination Council (CXC) Examination Body. They would definitely be in need of people with specialized expertise in psychometrics.

Consideration 2—UWI Professor Lawrence Reid, who constructed the Common Entrance Examinations Papers, was the only qualified person at the doctoral level in psychometrics in the Caribbean. I thought it was of strategic value and importance that I position myself to become his mentee and then his successor in that field.

These two considerations on reflection turned out to be my major practical experience in the development of one of the core competencies of a servant leader—strategic thinking—and one of the key attributes of a transformational leader—empowerment.

Having determined my programme of choice, the question as to my university of choice remained to be answered. My mentor, D.R.B. Grant, my former elementary school headmaster, recommended that the choice should be the University of Maryland (UM), College Park, USA. I agreed.

I had twelve days between receiving the offer of a scholarship and formally applying to UM and, upon acceptance, reporting to the university campus on time to start the first semester.

Senior officers in the MOE, such as the late Mr. Lennie Ruddock and the late Mr. Oswald Rutherford, advised me, as a government officer, to take advantage of the government services to facilitate and expedite some aspects of the process. I took their advice and did just that.

To make it all sound very official, I telephoned the dean at UM from the MOE office and told him to expect my application from the Embassy of Jamaica. I told him that the driver would wait until it was processed, together with the I20 Form, and would take these documents back to the Embassy of Jamaica.

This was my introduction to the diplomatic pouch, in which I sent the papers to the Embassy of Jamaica in Washington, DC. The information officer at the embassy at the time was Martin Mordecai. He played a key role in getting my application to UM, then having it returned to the embassy and then back to me in Jamaica—all in three days!

Having received my acceptance letter and I20 Form, I then started the process of obtaining my student visa.

In preparation for my visit to the US Embassy, I still remember the content, style, and structure of the letter written by Mrs. Ina Skyers, a manager at the Ministry of Education's head office.

This letter facilitated my getting a speedy response from the consular officer at the US Embassy.

Mrs. Skyers's professionalism, the pride she took in her role as a civil servant, and the value she placed on developing and utilizing effective written communication skills left a lasting impression on me.

After all these twists and turns, I entered the UM on time! Martin and I kept in close contact with each other after I arrived at UM.

The University of Maryland (UM) took me to another level of

understanding a different culture, furthering my experience with diversity management, affording me the opportunity to get a peek into international affairs, and teaching me important leadership lessons. Thus began another exciting part of my journey in becoming a servant leader.

The University of Maryland, College Park—the flagship among the state's institutions of higher learning—is one of the nation's preeminent public research universities. It is a global leader in research, entrepreneurship, and innovation, and is renowned for its programmes in academics, the arts, athletics, and social entrepreneurship.

Located just outside Washington, DC, the university is home to more than 41,000 students, 14,000 faculty and staff, and 388,000 alumni.

Self-Confidence, Self-Esteem, and Diversity Management

At UM, the faculty, staff, and student body were predominantly white. This, however, was not a factor in the university facilitating a strong sense of community and "oneness" among all groups. So I was not at all daunted by this overwhelming racial imbalance.

Indeed, I was confident in my Jamaican sense of "smaddyness" (being somebody) and deeply rooted in the cultural mindset of proud Jamaicans, who can take our place and make our mark anywhere in the world and against whatever background we are placed.

In addition, I knew that I was unquestionably the intellectual equal of the best students on the campus.

Being the son of a father of Chinese descent and a black mother of

African descent, I grew up living and operating from a positive position of value and self-worth, in spite of being socially endowed with titles of dubious honour, such as "Chiney-royal" and "Black-head-Chiney."

My self-esteem was never in jeopardy because of these epithets, nor were my character, creative thoughts, positive actions, and leadership capacity.

In addition, growing up in a segregated hometown where there were clear lines of distinction between rich and poor was good preparation for my UM sojourn.

The entry to UM made me acutely aware of the importance of the leadership skill of diversity management, which I started to learn in my boyhood years and developed further in high school at The Mico and UWI. Now I had the opportunity to hone this skill at UM.

On reflection, it also brought home to me, quite forcibly, that cumulative experiences play a critical role in shaping you as a servant leader.

At UM, I claimed and exhibited, even more forcibly, Marcus Garvey's mantra, "Emancipate yourself from mental slavery. None but ourselves can free our minds."

I was introduced to the life, work, and impact of Marcus Garvey by Marcus Junior, who was in my mathematics class at UWI for a year.

Years later, I met his son, who was also named Marcus Junior, and he was fascinated to hear me validate stories his father had told him of his prowess as a mathematician and a mathematics teacher at Kingston College and Kingston Technical High School.

I also later met Julius Garvey, the younger son of Marcus Mosiah Garvey, when we were both members of the Technical Committee of Experts Meeting on the African Diaspora, in South Africa. We continue to be good friends and professional colleagues.

A fellow Jamaican student at UM, Karl Wright (now Professor Karl Wright), a former student of Knox College, shared with me the following observations he had made about me while we were at UM:

9. "Despite cultural/ethnic differences, your UM professors and classmates, in time, overcame whatever initial biases they may have had against you and came to regard you as an exceptional student."

10.

11. "Though UM had very few nonwhite students, you would not allow that reality to impede your drive to excel."

12. "You became a role model and mentor for nonwhite and international students, and for many white students too!"

13. "In many ways, you were a trailblazer. It would be interesting to know how many, if any, black students—before and after you—earned a doctorate in measurement, statistics, and research designs from UM."

When I was an employee of Jamaica's Ministry of Education (MOE), Eric Budhlall and I worked together in the Inner Management Group. Eric was an economist and I was a mathematics specialist and educator.

We enjoyed many robust discussions between us, and we argued on differing points of view but always with the greatest respect for each other's position.

An important lesson I learnt from Eric was to set the target end date for completing an initiative and work backward from it! Thanks to Eric, when I arrived at UM, I applied this principle to good effect.

In my first weeks, I set my graduation date with my adviser and milestones for achieving this target date. My adviser said, "Neville, you are crazy!"

His reason for this comment was that I had shared with him my plan to complete both a master's and a doctoral degree in three years, the period covered by my scholarship!

My reply to my adviser was "That is my problem!"

His response was "You sound serious; let us get to work then!"

Well, together we worked, and he really pushed me and supported me toward the targeted end goal.

I am pleased and proud to share with you that, at the end of my three-year scholarship tenure at UM, I graduated with both my master's and doctoral degrees as planned.

Cultural Adaptability

It was while I was at UM that my understanding of the Jamaican diaspora and how its members survive and prosper in host countries was fully launched. I witnessed firsthand the resilience, work ethic, determination, and ambitions of my fellow Jamaicans.

I observed how they took full advantage of the multiple educational and economic opportunities the United States afforded them, and how they were bolstered by that unique and distinctive "Jamaicaness" that enabled them to undertake and overcome the odds, just pushing on through, in spite of the challenges, to achieve upward social and economic mobility.

This experience of being a member of the Jamaican diaspora gave me a unique vantage point for understanding the challenges and opportunities that this group encountered in a different cultural setting.

I therefore can speak with sensitivity and authority about the aspirations, achievements, contributions, issues, and concerns of this important group of Jamaicans who reside in host countries such as the United States.

It was good preparation for my future leadership role in engaging members of the Jamaican diaspora when I established and served as executive director of the Jamaica Diaspora Institute.

The Watergate scandal, which was a political scandal in the United States involving the administration of President Richard Nixon, from 1972 to 1974, started shortly after I arrived at UM and ended with his resignation the semester before I graduated.

UM College Park was in close proximity to Washington, DC, and I was able to follow the events of this historic period in US history daily. In the process, I learnt a lot about the American political system and its constitutional checks and balances.

Watergate also taught me a very important leadership lesson: no one, regardless of power or office, is above the law.

UM also had a very interesting ritual in my era. On the first day of spring, students would lay on their backs, next to each other, for about an hour on the lawns of the vast campus at College Park, looking up at the sky to welcome spring and say goodbye to winter. This ritual took place whether spring was ushered in with warm sunshine, warm showers, or a combination of both.

Then there were Saturday night sessions in the Coffee Room, where we listened to mood and message music, with selections from artistes such as Joan Baez, the Beatles, and Sam Cooke.

There were also the many and varied recreational activities such as bowling at the Student Union , having ice cream at the Dairy (the best ice cream in the Maryland and Washington, DC, area); watching a variety of intercollegiate sporting activities, including basketball (UM was in the USA's top two in my era), lacrosse, football, soccer, and lawn tennis.

I also set about learning American football (which is quite different from soccer and has features of rugby) and the various facets of the game—first down, touchdown, and the strategies related to each; the key role of the quarterback, special coaches, and game strategists on the sidelines; as well as other important elements of the game.

This made me feel even more comfortable with my new friends from the US, as I could now join in and share the excitement of these games with them.

These were very important leadership lessons in cultural adaptation. More significantly, these experiences taught me critical leadership skills you can learn from sports, such as planning, strategizing, and the importance of members of the team effectively performing the roles with which they are entrusted.

Servant Leadership Lesson

Cultural adaptability is important to be an effective leader in both a national and an international context.

My experiences at UM and its environs provided valuable immersion into a new culture and lessons in cultural adaptability, while maintaining my Jamaican identity.

In later years I found this to be important preparation for providing leadership in Jamaica, as well as in the Caribbean region and internationally.

Building a Network of Relationships

Through my UM experience, the value and the power of networking, especially leveraging alumni connections, was reinforced for me.

Lasting friendships were formed with other students with whom I studied and shared memorable moments—students who came from countries such as the US, Japan, Greece, Nigeria, China, Guyana, and Jamaica.

My first two weeks at UM were very interesting.

UM was informed that I was on a full government scholarship covering tuition, accommodations, and books. Thus, when I arrived, they booked me to stay at the Adult Center at a rate of ninety dollars US per night.

The only problem was that my funding from the government for accommodations would not arrive from New York for about two months, and all the money I had brought with me amounted to $300 US. Naturally, this was an economically untenable situation.

After the first night's stay at the Adult Center, I began to urgently seek far cheaper living quarters. I asked the receptionist to direct me to the Student Union where I hoped that I would meet a fellow student who would be looking for a roommate to share the expenses.

The receptionist, in directing me to the Student Union, advised me to take the bus. Between my precarious economic situation, however, and my experience at UWI, Mona Campus, I determined that the UM Student Union could not be so far away that I would need to take a bus.

So I set out walking. Big mistake.

Unknown to me then, the vastness of the UM College Park campus was no walk in the park and made the entire UWI, Mona Campus, which to me was quite expansive, seem like a mere garden path.

As I walked, and walked, and walked, the said bus that I should have taken passed me by—and I still had a very, very long walk left to get to my destination. This was my first culture shock.

I finally arrived at the Student Union and was further frustrated by my efforts at finding leads to more affordable lodging. I was forced then to continue for the second night at the expensive Adult Center.

On the third day, I was down to my last hundred dollars US.

As God would have it, a few days before I left for UM, Pat Stern came to visit her friend, Alberta Estwick, who was the minister's secretary at the MOE, while I was on staff there.

Pat and I had met many years earlier at one of the parties organized for Dinthill and Carron Hall students, when we both attended the respective schools, and who, serendipitously, had also enrolled as a student nurse at KPH while I was at The Mico.

It was quite a surprise and a joyous reunion to see her again after about ten long years.

We enquired of each other about our lives and occurrences in the intervening years. She shared with me the fact that she had gotten married, had two children, and now lived with her family in Maryland.

She was as surprised and excited as I was to learn that I would be going to Maryland in a few days as a UM student. She gave me her telephone number to contact her when I got there.

It was quite fortuitous, therefore, that I not only recalled our meeting and had her telephone number with me, but that I also was able to swallow my pride and reach out to her in desperation for assistance with my housing plight.

Pat received my call with a warm welcome and kind regard, and she graciously offered me lodging at her home. She cautioned, however, that I would have little or no privacy, given the fact that I would be sharing a three-bedroom house with her husband and two children.

With sincere gratitude for her generosity of spirit, I pooh-poohed her caution and humbly accepted her, undoubtedly, self-sacrificial offer. Her husband, Tony Morrison, came to pick me up that very day.

And so it was that during my first year at UM, I lived with my fellow Jamaicans and friends—Tony Morrison, who was a dental student at Howard University, and Pat Morrison, a registered nurse, along with their two children, Wayne and Kym, who became like my own children.

The Jamaican Embassy in Washington, DC, was also very supportive in providing me with an advance sum of money to help tide me over until my scholarship funds arrived. From that experience I developed a great respect and appreciation for our embassies and missions overseas.

I want to publicly record, in this publication, my deep appreciation and gratitude to two staff members at the Embassy of Jamaica at that time, who personally and .professionally extended themselves to see to my care. These two wonderful persons are Mrs. Joyce Phillips, who was like a mother to me, and Martin Mordecai, who was a very supportive friend.

Martin and his wife, Pam, contributed immensely to making my stay at UM enjoyable and memorable. We continued to enjoy a close relationship even after I left UM and returned home to Jamaica.

Martin, who was then an information officer at the Embassy of Jamaica, later became deputy high commissioner to Trinidad and Tobago. Again Martin, supported by his secretary, Sandra Grant-Griffith (now chief of protocol at the Office of the Prime Minister, OPM), took good care of me when I visited T&T on official MOE business.

My family was now preparing to join me in Maryland, so I needed new accommodations. I found a lovely two-bedroom, garden-type apartment, close to UM College Park. The only challenge was that the owners were very particular about the people to whom they rented these apartments.

My negotiation strategy was to call Martin at the Embassy of Jamaica and ask him to call and assure the rental office that I was a bona fide Government of Jamaica (GOJ) employee, and that funding was assured to cover my rental expenses.

Martin agreed to make the call, and with his "official" intervention, I got the apartment.

Life got better as time passed. The then minister of education, Florizel Glasspole, (who later became Sir Florizel Glasspole, governor general), wrote a beautiful letter to Robert Carbone, the dean of the faculty in the area I was studying.

In this letter, the minister indicated that the Ministry of Education supported the investment by the Government of Jamaica in my further training and development, and it appreciated UM's role in facilitating this mission. I still have a copy of this letter, which the dean gave to me.

After the receipt of that letter from the minister, I received special treatment at UM College Park. I could now enjoy special favours, such as having my own study room in the main library and having coffee in the staff lounge.

I also formed my own Diaspora Network of Jamaicans studying in the area. This included Jamaican students at Howard University, UM College Park, Georgetown University, and American University, as well as staff members at the Embassy of Jamaica in Washington, DC.

My friends from Howard University were mostly dental students. I had sessions where I helped them with statistics.

Some students had interesting ways of paying their way through university. One way they did this was to buy a car that doubled as their personal mode of transportation and a public taxi service.

Another was that each month a student would have a fee-paying rent party, the proceeds of which would go to pay the rent for that person's apartment.

The overhead expenses for these rent parties were low. The meal consisted of chicken that was chopped up "fine" (in small bits), curried, and served with rice. The drinks would be large portions of cheap Kool-Aid, mixed with a lot of water and served with plenty of ice.

Sometimes the beverage offering would be spiked with Jamaican rum punch on the side. One of our American friends who attended one of these parties was very concerned when the rum punch was finished.

Not knowing the formula for rum punch, he just threw a bottle of Jamaican 150 overproof white rum in a bowl with Hawaiian Punch. It was soon "lights-out" for a lot of high-spirited party people, shortly after imbibing the highly potent brew.

The music during these parties was a mix of Jamaican music—rock-steady, ska, and reggae—and American R and B. The playlist included some of my favourite hits, such as "Stir It Up," Bob Marley; "54-46 Was My Number," Toots and the Maytals; "Shanty Town," Desmond Decker and the Aces; "I Need a Roof," Mighty Diamonds; "Young, Gifted and Black," Bob Andy and Marcia Griffiths; "Blazing Fire," Derrick Morgan; "King of Kings," Jimmy Cliff; "Conversation," Slim Smith and the Uniques; "You Don't Care for Me," The Techniques; "I'm Stone in Love with You," Stylistics; "Here I Am" and "Let Us Stay Together," Al Green; "Never Gonna Give You Up," Barry White; "I Feel Good" and "This Is a Man's World," James Brown; "My Girl," the Temptations; "Under the Boardwalk," Drifters; and "After All Is Said and Done," O. C. Smith.

Leadership Lessons from Academic Pursuits

The late Professor Vernon Anderson, my first adviser at UM, taught me two important servant leadership lessons.

- **Servant Leadership Lesson 1**

Visioning is important to enable persons you serve to visualize future possibilities for their progress and success.

A vision is a practical guide for creating plans, setting goals and objectives, making decisions, and coordinating and evaluating the work on any project, large or small.

A powerful vision pulls in ideas, people, and other resources and inspires action. It creates the energy and will to make change happen.

The famous John Graham—adventurer, former Foreign Service officer, writer, speaker, political activist, and a leader of the Giraffe Heroes Project—expressed profound insight on the "Importance of Visioning" when he wrote this in his *Life on the Edge* blog:

A vision is a mental picture of the result you want to achieve. A picture so clear and strong it will help make that result real. A vision is not a vague wish or dream or hope. It's a picture of the real results of real efforts. It comes from the future and informs and energizes the present.

Professor Anderson's method of teaching us visioning was as follows:

He would conduct classes with his graduate students in a very relaxed setting at his home, where there would be tea and homemade cookies and cake served during these sessions.

In these sessions, he would bring together a dynamic fusion of students like me, who were in the first year of graduate school, with the more advanced class of doctoral-level students, who were nearing completion of their doctoral dissertation.

His aim was to provide first-year graduate students like me with a vision of where we could get to through consistent, hard, and smart work as was the case with the doctoral-level students.

Visioning is the most powerful tool I've used and seen demonstrated in later years while I helped organizations and individuals to visualize the future and develop and execute the roadmap to get the results they desired.

- **Servant Leadership Lesson 2**

It is important as a leader to use your core competencies to develop lasting friendships and support professional knowledge networks.

Core competencies are the defining characteristics that make an individual stand out and add value. Identifying and exploiting core competencies is seen as important for individuals to make their mark.

The sharing of knowledge, and the networks and professional activities developed to enable knowledge sharing, are essential for the ongoing development of professionals and organizations.

Professor Anderson understood, facilitated, and promoted the value of a knowledge-sharing culture.

During sessions with graduate students at his home, he found out that I was strong in the area of statistics. As a result, he would encourage the students who were nearing the end of their doctoral programme to get assistance from me in this area.

One of these doctoral candidates called me early one morning, at about seven o'clock. He said to me, "I had the defense of my thesis, and I was sent back to improve my statistical analysis. I have been up since four o'clock looking at the figures, and they don't make any sense to me."

My advice to him was "If you continue looking at them, they still won't make any sense. Go and get some sleep and meet me in the library at ten thirty."

We met as planned, and I assisted him with his statistical analysis. He returned to his oral examinations and successfully defended his thesis.

This intervention and other knowledge-sharing interactions with graduate students in Professor Anderson's class launched for me the formation of a very valuable network of professionals in the Maryland and Washington, DC, area.

This network proved to be quite invaluable throughout my course of study and continued even after I returned to Jamaica to subsequent leadership, management, and academic positions.

The late Dr. John Giblette, who was my adviser for my doctoral research and dissertation, taught me an important servant leadership lesson.

- **Servant Leadership Lesson 3**

It is important as a leader to differentiate between your role and the role of others and the value of the combination of these roles.

Dr Giblette was very insistent and would strongly emphasize the point that when I returned to the world of work, I should not focus on doing "statistical computations." Those were tasks I should assign to people that I supervise.

My focus should be on "analysis and interpretation of data" to provide information to make important policy and strategic decisions for the organization.

Dr. Craig Scott who supervised me during my doctoral internship in Fredrick County, Maryland, also taught me an important servant leadership lesson.

- **Servant Leadership Lesson 4**

If the people you serve don't understand and relate to what you are saying as a leader, they will not buy into the vision that you are inviting them to share and be excited about.

The research for my doctoral dissertation focused on factors that impact a student's performance in subjects such as mathematics and English. These include the way in which we pose questions to students in different tests, their level of intelligence, and their gender and socioeconomic status.

Just for the record, notice the difference between my explanation above and the technical title of my dissertation, which was

"Parallel Measures as a Function of Response Formats: An Experimental Investigation of the Effects of Response Formats on the Constancy of Variances, Covariances, and Group Mean Scores."

Dr. Scott was fascinated by my areas of investigation and asked me to give a presentation to the Board of Education for the county. I took this important assignment very seriously.

I prepared a very technical presentation, including the use of different research designs and the statistical applications, such as a multivariate analysis.

Thankfully I had the humility and foresight to ask Dr. Scott to review what I had prepared before my actual presentation.

The summary of his review and subsequent critique was "Neville, in the real world, people are only interested in and understand average and percentage."

I have never forgotten his very forthright and profound response. The result was that in all future technical presentations, including the one for the Board of Education for the county, I have focused primarily on the two critical areas of *averages* and *percentages*.

For averages, I drill down what I am communicating to examples such as average salary in a firm, mean score of a student on different examinations, etc.

For percentages, I would, for example, speak about the percentage (%) of persons who like the product a company is selling, the percentage (%) of persons who will vote for a political party, or the percentage (%) score of a student on an examination, etc.

Another very important experience for me at UM was being afforded the opportunity to participate, for the first time in my life, as a presenter at an international conference.

- **Servant Leadership Lesson 5**

Strategic thinking and team building are important competencies for a servant leader to acquire.

One of my professors while I was doing graduate research was Dr. Louise Berman, author of *New Priorities in the Curriculum* (1968).

Her focus in this book was on the process-oriented person. She stressed the importance of the following processes in teaching and learning: perceiving, knowing, communicating, loving, patterning, decision-making, creating, and valuing.

I was fascinated with this approach to curriculum development, together with teaching and learning.

On reflection, I realize that exposure to these human development processes were important building blocks for shaping my leadership competencies in strategic thinking and team building.

Dr. Berman invited me to join her at the Association for Supervision and Curriculum Development (ASCD) Conference in Minneapolis.

As a graduate student, I thought that I was going with her to ensure that her presentation materials were prepared and her audio-visual equipment was in order.

To my surprise, while on the flight en route to the conference, she told me I would be copresenting with her. This was an alarming development. It was both an exciting and truly frightening contemplation—the prospect of speaking to an international audience of over one thousand people!

I believe God must have clearly been with me, for as I disembarked the plane in Minneapolis, the first person I saw was Billy Graham.

I knew that this sighting of the world-renowned and revered evangelist must have been a sign from God that He was with me and all would be well.

You see, for years in Jamaica, I listened to Billy Graham on the radio, introducing his programme by saying, "This is Billy Graham, Minneapolis, Minnesota."

My presentation went over well and was acclaimed as a huge success.

A representative from the Organization of American States (OAS), who was in attendance at the conference, made a point of congratulating me on the presentation. She went further to invite me to visit her at the OAS office in Washington, DC.

The office was just a short drive from UM. I went to see her, and she informed me that it was her intention to recommend me for an OAS scholarship. Regrettably, I had to refuse the offer because I was already on a government scholarship.

That experience, as with all my experiences at UM, was truly memorable and impactful, and is indelibly etched in my mind.

The combined MICO, UWI, and UM experiences and exposures provided an excellent preparatory foundation for my work and service as a servant leader in Jamaica, regionally (CARICOM), and internationally.

This was especially so for my years of service, in a leadership capacity, in organizations such as the Overseas Examinations Commission (OEC), the University Council of Jamaica, the International Labour Organization (ILO) in Geneva, United Nations activities in Denmark and Brazil, the Caribbean Examination Council (CXC), the Caribbean Employers Confederation (CEC), and the Business Schools of UWI.

Many, like me, have gained tremendously from all the institutions of learning, at all educational levels, that we have had the great privilege and benefit of attending.

I arrived at each school, college, or university ready and willing to embark on an incredible journey of scholarship and intellectual development and other learning experiences.

It quickly became a revelation that to truly optimize the myriad benefits and enhance the impact of the many dynamic learning experiences is to use them as important building blocks in your development as a servant leader.

My college and university experiences have reinforced valuable leadership lessons and life skills through my classes and extracurricular activities, and I have been truly strengthened in my capacity and my resolve to be a deeply motivated and effective servant leader.

There is no one model for effective leadership. Our styles, methods, and approaches to the challenges are influenced at so many levels by many variables. Our leadership response is completely dependent upon our understanding and navigation of the culture and politics of the context of the challenge.

It is arguable as to whether or not education is a critical arbiter in determining leadership quality. It may well be that the notion of "the best and the brightest" as a vital factor in the leadership quality equation is of little value.

What is inarguable, however, is that it would be a mistake to rule out the many positive examples of the outcome and impact of education on leadership quality.

I find it instructive to end this chapter on these two quotes:

The function of education, therefore, is to teach one to think intensively and to think critically. Intelligence plus character—that is the goal of true education.—Martin Luther King Jr.

I have been impressed with the urgency of doing. Knowing is not enough; we must apply. Being willing is not enough; we must do.

—Leonardo da Vinci

7

Employing the Servant Leader:
Stories, Lessons, and Impact of the World of Work: Teaching and Administration

> Leadership is about making others better
> as a result of your presence
> and making sure that impact lasts in your absence.
> —Sheryl Sandberg

THE FIRST PHASE of my early working career started immediately after I left The Mico when I was engaged in teaching at two schools in inner-city communities.

The second phase was after I graduated from UWI and returned to The Mico as a lecturer.

The third phase was prior to attending the University of Maryland. I moved on from The Mico to join the civil service as an officer at the Ministry of Education (MOE).

These phases represented an important blend of moving to and from theory to practice in shaping me as a servant leader. In each of these phases of my early working life, I learnt many important lessons that formed important components of shaping me as a servant leader.

The details of these phases are as follows:

Early Years of Teaching—Moving from Theory to Practice

After graduation from The Mico, my early years as a trained teacher started at Denham Town School and then St, Andrew Technical High School (STATHS). Both schools are located in West Kingston.

The geographic spread of West Kingston took me from Coronation Market in the east, to Bumper Hall in the west, with Back O Wall (now Tivoli Gardens) and May Pen Cemetery in between. It included Denham Town, Trench Town, Jones Town, and other areas.

Starting my teaching in this part of Jamaica was not my choice. I had little say in the decision about where I would be deployed to teach. I was, however, willing and ready to go wherever I was sent.

As it turned out, teaching in the schools to which I was assigned, and working in the communities in which they were located, proved to be one of the most enriching and empowering sets of experiences in my teaching career and my development as a servant leader.

It facilitated the provision of an early training ground in understanding, among other critical things, the socioeconomic dynamics of inner-city communities, with all their unique challenges and volatility, and the intellectual capacity, competencies, and creativity of its residents.

In addition, and perhaps most importantly, my own socioeconomic background as a youngster prepared me to be not only sensitive to the personal and environmental realities of my students, but also to extend myself beyond teaching to become an empowering influence in their lives.

So how did I get to be selected for schools in West Kingston?

Well, about a month before my graduation from The Mico, my mentor, D.R.B. Grant (headmaster of my former elementary school), brought some forms for me to sign.

I duly signed the forms as instructed, after which he informed me that I would be teaching at Denham Town School as of the first of September. He also told me that I would be working under the tutelage of Mr. W.B.C. Hawthorne, veteran educator.

I was further advised by D.R.B. that he had arranged for me to board with one of his batch mates from The Mico, Mr. Whitworth, who lived at 11½ Chalmers Avenue, St. Andrew.

Of interest was that D.R.B. Grant's wife, Gene, attended Bethlehem Teachers' College with Mr Whitworth's wife. So both families were closely bonded with each other on all sides.

Mrs. Whitworth was the "lady of the house," with her husband and four sons. I, too—along with another male boarder, Claude Robinson—became one of the family, and her sons became our brothers. Leo was the eldest; Tony the second; Barry, aka Cal, the third; and Horace, aka Babes, the youngest.

One side of the house became known as the "Kingston College (KC) side" because all the boys attended KC, except Barry, who attended Jamaica College (JC). I, along with Claude, who was then deputy head boy at Calabar High School and became my lifelong friend, occupied the front room.

This front room was located on the short side of the house, known as the "Calabar side," due to Claude's connection with the school. I had pride of place there because I was a young teacher from The Mico.

You can only imagine the long, loud, and robust arguments between us, especially during the week of Boys Champs, Jamaica's premier schools' track and field championships, which were then held at Sabina Park.

The boys were allowed to go anywhere on a Saturday afternoon as long as they were going out with me. Their mother regarded me as a responsible young man who would take care of her dearly beloved "charges." I did not let her down.

Claude was old enough to go with me to Sombrero Club, located on Molynes Road. We especially liked to go there on Thursday evenings when there was special music and curried goat was the main item on the menu.

I also spent time listening to Claude practicing to read the news as if he was on the radio station. Little wonder then, that in later years, he became the prime minister's press secretary and, at one time, general manager of the powerful radio and television media house, Jamaica Broadcasting Corporation (JBC). Today, he is highly regarded and widely respected as a veteran journalist and media commentator.

For me, and, I believe, for all of us in the Whitworth household, this was a most exciting, enjoyable, and comfortable boarding arrangement. With the Whitworths I found a new warm, loving, and caring family, and together we were as one, without countenance to the absence of blood ties.

In those days especially, mentors took their roles seriously. In addition to the financial assistance they gave their mentees, mentors gave their mentees a "push start" in their careers. Mentors also taught their mentees sound principles and values, such as trustworthiness and reliability.

They also taught and demonstrated the importance of using their influence and network to facilitate the development and careers of their mentees.

To launch me on my teaching career, D.R.B. Grant gave me twenty pounds as a loan to buy clothes and other items so I would look dignified as a new teacher. His instructions were that I should pay back this amount over the next twelve months by taking each monthly installment to another of his MICO batch mates, Laurie Reid.

At the end of each month, therefore, my first two commitments were paying for boarding at the Whitworths and taking my monthly payment to Laurie Reid in Richmond Park.

Laurie, in later years, progressed to become Professor Laurie Reid, psychometrician. He also became my mentor when I later served as the Caribbean Examination Council (CXC)'s technical adviser in measurement and evaluation.

Teaching at Denham Town School started out as a challenging experience.

During my final year in college, I wrote a prize-winning essay on the topic "Don't Spare the Rod and Spoil the Child." In this essay I put forward strong arguments based on educational research that teachers should not engage in administering corporal punishment.

I quickly learnt the difference between theory and practice.

I was given a class of about sixty students, whose main mission it seemed was to frustrate me with their bad behaviour.

After a month or so of trying unsuccessfully to cope and effectively deal with this situation, I chose to forget about what I had posited in my award-winning essay, which opposed the use of corporal punishment as discipline in schools.

I took the bus to King Street, in downtown Kingston, and declared my intention with the purchase of a cane at the Times Store.

Armed with renewed energy and authority, I entered the classroom with grim determination to subdue any real or imagined tyranny against civility and good order. The use of my new acquisition spoke more forcibly and yielded far greater disciplinary results than my words ever could.

Or so I thought…

With each lash of the cane, the students began to quiet down, and I was assured of the success of the new measures. All seemed fine until one day I came to the startling and life-threatening realization that outside the classroom, where the cane had no jurisdiction, I was a vulnerable target for pent-up hurt and resentment.

This was manifested one day when, as I walked between two classrooms, stones came at me fast and furious, whistling past my head and thudding on the ground beyond. One of the boys, no doubt a hapless victim of my "cane of command" in the classroom, was unleashing his fury at me and trying to stone me out of the school.

Far from being stoned out of my mind by the threat of what was happening, in a kind of reflex action, the skill and mastery of mango-stoning in my boyhood days sprung to mind, and no time was lost between thought and action as I started flinging rock stones back at this boy, forcing him to beat a hasty retreat from the schoolyard.

That was the first incident.

The second incident involved a boy who, in a vicious fight, was putting a neck hold on another boy so tightly that he was about to strangle him to death. When I came upon the scene, my immediate response was to thump the offender very hard, which forced him to release his potentially murderous grip on the other boy's neck.

These incidents challenged my creative, solutions-driven thinking.

I wanted to remain true to my commitment to be a professional and effective teacher, and an empowering and transformational leader, but the situations with which I was faced challenged those commitments.

I decided then and there that I must find and employ other strategies for dealing with adverse behavioural and other issues in schools and, by extension, communities.

This search for strategic solutions led to my learning about, and engaging with, the power of sports as an agent for positive behavioural change.

You will recall that in addition to being a specialist in mathematics and physics in college, I also specialized in sports and physical education.

Again fortuitously, as so often happened along my journey through life, four of us who specialized in sports and physical education taught at Denham Town School and other schools in nearby areas.

Cecil Dinnall and I were at Denham Town, Bill Brown at Boys Town, and Sexton Hope at Cockburn Pen.

We pooled our skills and started a serious Sports Development Programme at the institutions where we worked, focusing initially on cricket, football, and volleyball, which was just gaining popularity in Jamaica.

We also organized competitions in these areas of sports among the boys and girls from our respective institutions.

The *Daily Gleaner* published an article on July 5, 2016, headlined, "The Impact of Physical Education and Sport." The writer, Jennifer Ellison Brown, wrote in part:

> The findings of a group of studies indicated that participation

in sport increased students' overall interest and commitment to schooling, as well as their engagement in more student-teacher contact, more positive attitudes about schooling, and more parent-school contact.

This powerful strategic approach enabled the development of a new type of student/teacher relationship. In addition to this, we started getting to know the parents, guardians, and other members of the different communities.

We took this to another level, however, and moved beyond sports to include other social and recreational activities, all designed to strengthen and deepen our interaction and relationships with each other.

Some of my students whom I got to know well included Lloyd and Linden Wright, the brothers of Collie Smith, the famous West Indies cricketer. Linden later became president of the Jamaica Cricket Association.

Other activities we engaged in included walking with our students during the day, or at night, from where North Street meets Spanish Road, all along North Street, and ending up at Sabina Park to watch a cricket match. Then we accompanied them to where they lived and returned by bus to where we lived.

We also sometimes watched movies and stage shows at Queens, Majestic, and Ambassador (Bass) Theatres in these areas.

We came to know after some time that we were protected as we walked through these otherwise threatening areas.

I learnt, for instance, that when I walked through these different communities and someone shouted loudly, "Mr. Ying!" or "Teach!" that this was a code to say "You are OK!" or "You are safe!" or "No one will touch/harm you!"

We didn't know it then, but what we were doing is what we now call school-community relationships in teacher education, leadership courses, and the leadership roles of teachers and principals in this process.

In doing what we were doing then, there were some important lessons to be learnt.

Lesson 1: *Get to know and interact with your students and build relationships with them outside of the regular classroom time, through a range of cocurricular activities.* This will carry over and influence an improved quality relationship with them in the classroom.

Lesson 2: *Get to know the parents and guardians of the children you teach*, and they will build a supporting relationship with you as a teacher in the interest of their child's development.

Lesson 3: *Spend time in the communities in which your students live.* This will have a positive impact on their attitude and capacity to learn in the formal classroom.

Lesson 4: *The transformational power of building soft skills is immeasurable.* It is important, therefore, that teachers place strong focus on building students' personal life skills, such as self-confidence, positive mental attitude, ability to work and play as a team and not as individuals, and development of a balanced disposition.

Teaching skills and/or methodologies of a sport or subject area is important. The truth, however, is this should be combined with the soft skills, such a self-confidence and teamwork, to enable students to optimize performance and the quality of their experiences on the playing field or in the classroom.

An event that brought this home to me was taking the first girls' volleyball team from a school in West Kingston to play at the YMCA.

My best players played poorly. After the match and discussions with them, I found out that it was the first time some of them were playing outside of their community and at a venue like the YMCA, which was then located in the "uptown" area of New Kingston. They were scared by the newness of it all and overwhelmed by the unfamiliarity of their surroundings.

When I found out what the issue was, I committed more time to building their self-esteem and mental attitude. This empowered them to grow from strength to strength, and they later went on a winning streak and became the "team to beat" wherever they played. They were totally transformed into being a champion team.

So what happened to my cane?

I am pleased to report that after my regrettable use (for about two months or so) of the dastardly instrument of torture, disguised as "discipline," I never used it again or engaged in any form of corporal punishment throughout the remainder of my teaching career.

In fact, I became, and remain, a strong advocate against the use of corporal punishment in schools, in homes…or elsewhere.

My experiences at Denham Town School were good preparation for performing a key leadership role in later years as founding director of the Multicare Foundation (MCF). The foundation was established in April 1993 under the theme of "Creating Hope, Empowering Many," and with endowments from the ICD Group Limited, LIME (then Cable & Wireless Jamaica Limited), and the Caribbean Cement Company Limited.

Essentially, the MCF sought to effect change in antisocial behaviour and the propensity to engage in violence-prone behaviours, in inner-city communities in East, Central, and West Kingston through the use of sports and the visual and performing arts.

Using my training in science subjects, my next strategic initiative was geared toward setting up the first science lab at the school.

I was even more emboldened to do so by the success of my negotiation skills in securing the agreement of the home economics teacher to allow us to use part of the home economics room in which to set up the lab.

I went to the Jamaica Information Service (JIS) and asked for some film strips on science. I then asked another company for a projector to show the film strips and yet another (Facey Pharmaceutical Division) for used test tubes. I soaked these secondhand test tubes in acid until they were like new again!

Of note is that years later, I became corporate vice president of the ICD Group of companies, of which Facey Commodity Limited was one of their largest subsidiaries, and the Pharmaceutical Division, one of the four divisions of the company.

With the lab now established, I set to work to "turn on" my students to the world of science and scientific explorations through experiments in a science laboratory.

I also had the opportunity to teach evening classes, tutoring students for the Third Jamaica Local Examination. This was a very successful venture.

In performing my mentorship role, I encouraged some of my students to enter the teaching profession. Three of them did after successful completion of the Third Jamaica Local Examination— Adolph Cameron and Winston Carroo, who pursued a programme of studies at The Mico; and Thelma Drake, who pursued her programme at St. Joseph's Teachers' College. Dr. Adolf Cameron later served with distinction as the general secretary of the Jamaica Teachers Association (JTA). Winston Carroo, who won The Mico Cornell Scholarship, became an international consultant in agriculture, and Thelma Drake, after an outstanding teaching stint in Jamaica, continued her teaching career in Florida, USA.

The next part of the journey in my early teaching career was at St. Andrew Technical High School (STATHS).

St. Andrew Technical High School (STATHS) opened at Bumper Hall as a new school. Mr. John Austin Holmes was the first principal of the school.

The school advertised for a physics teacher. I applied and got the job. The physics lab was not yet completed, however, so the principal asked me to choose another subject I could teach until the lab was ready. I chose to teach mathematics, and he agreed.

I became a pioneer teacher of mathematics at STATHS. This was the beginning of (if I may say so myself) a brilliant career as an outstanding mathematics teacher and mathematics educator.

The big challenge was that I was given a class that was repeating its second year. For about the first two weeks, no one in the class listened to me. Instead they made jokes and threw paper planes.

I zipped into my Denham Town gear and recalled the lessons learnt from my experiences there. So I took off my tie and joined in sharing some jokes as well…and no, I didn't make or throw paper planes!

At the end of the second week, the ground was sufficiently softened to facilitate meaningful conversation between us. The essence of what they disclosed was that they were told that they were "no good," and they believed it.

Upon hearing this, the lessons from my psychology classes at The Mico came to the fore, and propelled by that knowledge, I made a deal with them: "How would you like to prove all the people who said you are no good wrong ?" They all agreed!

I then dug deep into my unorthodox creative thinking mode.

I told the principal that I would not write any weekly lesson plans, but I would instead give him my teaching and learning plan for the year.

This plan consisted of analyzing the syllabus for the year and identifying key mathematical concepts. I would teach these key concepts for six months, teach the syllabus for three months, and spend two months coaching them for doing examinations.

My big challenge with that approach was to convince the principal to accept it.

So let me share with you some background information on the principal.

Mr. John Austin Holmes (JAH) had the great distinction of being the founding principal of STATHS, a position and role he valued highly and honoured with equal distinction.

With his brilliant combination of engineering, management, and pedagogical skills, he laid a solid foundation for the school and put STATHS on the map, so to speak.

I found out that students' performance in mathematics was of fundamental importance to an experiment on which Principal Holmes was embarking.

In this experiment, only the top students in English, Spanish, and mathematics could opt for the secretarial programme. His aim was to produce bilingual secretaries who were equally sound in the core subjects of mathematics and English.

The result was that students from that programme were in high demand in the private sector.

With the successful execution of pioneering experiments like these, Principal Holmes earned his stripes as an impressive transformational leader in education, who was innovative and fearless in his quest to create new paradigms in teaching and learning, and to chart new career paths for students.

He demonstrated the gradual shift away from the perception that technical-vocational (tech-voc) subjects were only for those who were not academically inclined and were more suited to hands-on technical skills.

Instead, he advocated for and operated from the more enlightened position that tech-voc education should involve an effective combination of high performance in core subjects such as mathematics and English, with high performance in technical subjects such as engineering, drawing, welding, electrical installation, home economics, typing, and shorthand.

As a graduate of a technical high school (Dinthill), I could easily understand and embrace the importance and relevance of this approach.

Principal Holmes's bold perspectives and actions in stimulating a kind of "education renaissance," which was taking place at that time in Jamaica and elsewhere across the Caribbean region and the world, resonated well with me.

I was at that early stage of my teaching career when I was emboldened and wanted support to demonstrate my own dynamic and innovative approaches to teaching and learning.

In this context, I felt comfortable in putting forward to Principal Holmes, for his approval, my new methodology for teaching mathematics.

The principal agreed, on the condition that my job would be at stake if I did not deliver the expected results. I was confident I would not fail.

Consequently, this methodology was approved and implemented.

The class did progressively well each year, with the end result being a brilliant 95 percent pass rate in the General Certificate Examinations (GCE).

Servant Leadership Lesson

As a servant leader, be willing to take risks—personal and professional—and challenge the status quo, but deliver on what you promised.

Consequently I never taught physics, even though I was interested in doing so, because the principal insisted that I remain the mathematics teacher.

In addition to my teaching methodology for mathematics, I engaged with students in sports, music, and drama.

I also employed similar strategic initiatives to what I did at Denham Town in order to facilitate building closer and stronger relationships with students and enabling effective teaching and learning.

I got to know details such as students who came to school without breakfast and no money for lunch, and students who had one uniform that they would wash and iron each night and wear to school the next day. I worked with the principal and staff to set up a welfare programme to assist these students.

I recommended that the most troublesome student be appointed head boy. He proved to be the best head boy the school had ever had.

There was a student who came to me in desperation because, due to his consistently unacceptable behaviour, the principal and teachers refused to sign the forms for him to sit for the GCE Examinations.

I agreed to sign the forms, and the student was allowed to take the exams.

This student did so well in the exams, he won three scholarships! One to the College of Arts, Science and Technology (CAST, now UTECH); one to The Mico; and the third to complete his bachelor's and master's degrees at a university in the United States.

He later returned as a teacher to his alma mater (STATHS).

When he went back to teach at STATHS, I got together with him and reminded him that he was not in a position to punish any students who gave him trouble, given his notorious though eventual glorious past with the institution. We had a good laugh on the matter. It was both gratifying and satisfying to see him choosing to become a professional teacher and setting high standards for his students in performance on examinations, as well as in behaviour.

Underpinning all that, he exhibited a caring, understanding, and empowering leadership character, which benefitted the school community and beyond.

He eventually moved on from teaching at STATHS to further training, and he became a pilot for Air Jamaica. This student was the late Carlton (C. C.) Campbell.

As a young teacher, I considered it to be a great advantage not to be able to afford a car. I took the bus with some of my students and walked with them from Spanish Road into the school compound each day. This was another opportunity for me to get to know them outside the formal classroom.

Key Lesson

Spend time knowing and engaging students outside the formal classroom setting.

I was house master for a house that, on paper, should have earned only the third-place position on Sports Day. Students earned points for placing first, second, third, or fourth position in an event.

I did the math on the events, and the calculations showed that if the house earned points in every event, the house could win by one point.

I called a meeting with our track and field team, and gave each member a responsibility. Some persons should come in first or second, and I just needed others to place third or fourth in their respective event.

On Sports Day, the team went out on the field and executed the plan. We won by two points because one member who was earmarked to place fourth in an event actually placed third!

This outcome proved to be a game-changer and boosted the morale of the team so that they placed first in subsequent events!

One of those winning students on my house team was the late Michael Fray, who was a great sprinter and later became an Olympian.

Of note is that some of the other teachers would often ask me how my students were so quiet and attentive in class. My answer was always "Because they have already made noise on the playing field!"

Key Lesson

Teach students important life skills such as teamwork, team spirit, and the responsibility of each team member to perform with excellence in whatever role they are assigned.

I also met interesting and talented teachers at STATHS who made my sojourn there exciting, productive, enjoyable, and a great professional development experience.

These teachers included Gilda Barracks (music), Hyacinth Kerr (shorthand and typed transcription), Mavis Creary and Joyce Hetram (Spanish), Mr. Wilkins (technical drawing), Madge Facey and Gene Grant (home economics), Marion Cousins (science), Inez Ellington (English), Lawton Wallace (art and volleyball), and Danny Arms (football).

One other teacher who stood out in my mind was my friend the late Trevor Rhone. Each day we would engage in intense discussions at lunchtime. One frequently discussed topic between us was about him leaving the teaching profession to write plays for a living full-time.

Of course I thought he was crazy, and he thought the same about me and my method of teaching mathematics.

The rest is history. Trevor became one of Jamaica's leading playwrights with plays such as *Old Story Time,* and he did screenwriting for the iconic movies *Smile Orange* and *The Harder They Come.*

We both excelled in those areas that we were passionate about.

One year, I was invited by the STATHS Alumni in New York to be the guest speaker at their fundraising function for their alma mater. I was treated royally and was delighted to be with everyone, which included, among others, two of my former students—Dr. Ron Ingleton and Bernadette Lee.

In my speech, I shared some of the stories about my experiences teaching and engaging with students. They were amazed that as a young teacher I was so aware of the challenges that they, as students, had endured in their personal and school life.

Through the years, I have had great encounters with some of my former students, many of whom went on to be outstanding leaders and professionals in their chosen field of endeavour.

Some of these students include Ron Escoffrey, who became an outstanding Realtor in the USA. Another is Silvera Castro, who, for many years, served as chairman of the board at STATHS, as well as chairman of the Jamaica Cultural Development Commission (JCDC), JCDC's Emancipation and Independence events, and the Festival Queen Committee.

As an interesting aside, Silvera and his brother outdanced Chubby Checker, the famous American rock and roll singer and dancer. They were participants in the JBC Teen Age Dance Party *(TADP)*

Chubby Checker was the featured live guest on the show, singing and dancing to his hit song "Let's Twist Again." Silvera and his brother "out-twisted" him in dance moves!

In my early years of teaching I encountered many experiences and interacted with so many people, which enabled me to develop the greatest respect for people from all walks of life and different circumstances.

My teaching experience at Denham Town and STATHS, which were schools in inner-city communities, was an important part of my journey in being shaped as a servant leader.

The servant leadership lessons I learnt were invaluable to me later in my working life and when I had the opportunity to perform servant leadership roles in a variety of organizations.

The following are some major ones:

Servant Leadership Lessons

Lesson 1: *As a servant leader, do not make assumptions about the talents of persons you serve based on your biases related to the communities in which they were born and raised.*

Lesson 2: *Mentorship is an important part of your role as a servant leader in building the self-esteem and self-confidence of the people you serve.*

Lesson 3: *As a servant leader challenge the status quo, but at the same time come up with creative ideas and innovative actions that can positively transform what you are challenging.*

Lesson 4: *When performing your servant leadership roles, give focused attention to teamwork and collaboration among the people you serve.*

Lesson 5: *Spend time getting to know the people you serve in both formal and informal settings and situations.*

Lesson 6: *Understanding the needs, challenges, and concerns of the people you serve provides an important platform for demonstrating genuine care for them.*

The Mico: Higher Education Work Experience

Before my graduation from UWI, and a month before my final examinations, Freddie Green, my former lecturer, recommended me to

The Mico as a candidate for the post of lecturer in physical education and sports.

Mr. Glen Owen, the then principal, came to the UWI campus and interviewed me. He offered me the job at The Mico because I would bring to the table the added value of being able to teach mathematics and physics.

I accepted the offer and joined the faculty at The Mico, with a teaching portfolio of three subjects—mathematics, physics, and physical education and sports.

Some of my colleague faculty members in the area of sports and physical education included Horace Lewis, whose dormitory space I shared while we were both at The Mico; Barbara Requa of National Dance Theatre Company (NDTC) fame; and Edith Allen, who transferred from The Mico Practicing School to teach at the college.

All together, these individuals made my work in this department enjoyable and productive.

I learnt and honed an important servant leadership lesson during my work experience at The Mico.

Servant Leadership Lesson

As a servant leader it is important that you build a network of friends and supporting professionals who will be of strategic value to you in the future.

I formed lasting friendships and professional relationships with several persons during my tenure at The Mico.

Two of these friendships, as you learnt in the previous chapter, proved to be of strategic value and importance to my admission and stay at the University of Maryland.

A number of young graduates from UWI joined the faculty at The Mico at the same time I did.

One of them was Pam Hitchen, who taught English. She and Martin Mordecai, who was then studying at UWI, got married close to her taking up the position at The Mico. Shortly thereafter, they had their first child, which also heralded the beginning of a long and enduring friendship between us.

There were times when the family's helper did not turn up for work, so Pam had to stay home to take care of the young baby. On those days, I sat in for her in her English class to avoid the principal missing her.

I was, incidentally, a fairly good teacher of English and had, in fact, done quite well in Latin and literature in my studies at college. I may even have chosen to specialize in those subject areas had mathematics and physics not consumed my interest so completely.

Back then at The Mico, I was young, energetic, and physically and mentally fit. On a typical day I would teach physical education and sport, have a shower, change clothes, take a break, teach mathematics, have lunch, teach physics…and then head back to the playing field for sports practice sessions.

Jeremy Palmer, a former member of Parliament and now a prominent lawyer, was one of my mathematics students at The Mico. Jeremy, in later years, was a director of the board of Mico University College, during my tenure as chairman of the board.

His legal expertise was invaluable in helping me deal with policy and governance issues.

He reminded me of an amusing incident about the time I first walked into their class to deliver my lecture in mathematics.

I was so young that he and all the other students in the class thought I was a student "grub" (freshman), who had arrived late to the college. They were all getting set to "rag" (akin to American "haze") me.

Their "villainous" intentions were thwarted when, to their great surprise, I greeted them confidently and introduced myself as their lecturer in mathematics...and that put paid to that!

I enjoyed teaching mathematics—especially because I was fascinated with "new maths" or "new mathematics," which was a dramatic change in the way mathematics was taught. New maths involved the use of the "number line" and Sets to excite both students and teachers. It was also gaining popularity in the Jamaican curriculum.

This was excellent preparation for the next phase of my early working career.

The Ministry of Education (MOE) Work Experience from Teaching to Administration

My role as a lecturer in mathematics at The Mico laid the foundation for the launch of my new career as a civil servant.

My next stop then on my journey to UM was mathematics officer at the Ministry of Education (MOE).

I applied for a job as a mathematics officer with the MOE and was interviewed for the position by Euclid King, senior education officer.

I had met Euclid when I taught mathematics at St. Andrew Technical High School (STATHS). He had just returned home to Jamaica after completing his master's degree in mathematics, and he worked in my stead while I was on one month's leave of absence.

Euclid was not one for having long meetings and was very terse in communicating his analysis of situations and related solution strategies. The interview was therefore brief.

He asked me, "Can you start on the first of September?"

I said, "Yes."

He said, "OK."

And that was that! The end of the interview.

So on the first of September that year, I joined the staff of the Ministry of Education (MOE).

My first tour of duty with the MOE was working with Dr. Phyllis McPherson of the UWI's Institute of Education (IOE) and Mr. Hugh Moss-Solomon of the MOE. They were both excellent and experienced mathematicians and mathematics educators in the joint (UWI/MOE) Institute of Education's Mathematics Project.

The mathematics project sought to improve the teaching and learning of mathematics in all educational institutions across Jamaica. I became codirector with them for the project.

The United States supported the project by providing a cadre of Peace Corp volunteers, who were all young college graduates.

Prior to being selected to assist teachers in Jamaica under the mathematics project, the volunteers had to pursue a six-week Teacher Training Programme in Mathematics, which was organized for them in San Diego, California.

About six months after I joined the MOE, Mr. Moss-Solomon, who was scheduled to conduct the Teacher Training Programme in San Diego, was forced to decline, due to the sudden illness of his mother. I was recommended to take his place.

I was now thrown into the deep end, so to speak.

This was the first time in my life I was getting an opportunity to travel outside of Jamaica. I did not have a passport, but by virtue of being a civil servant, I was able to get one very quickly. A few days later, I was given a five-year, multiple-entry visa to the USA.

I arrived in San Diego on a Sunday, and the following day I was informed in a meeting with the programme coordinator that he needed my six-week programme plan and budget in two days' time.

I had never prepared any documents of this kind before. I set to work, however, and applied my mathematical skills, knowledge from my education courses in college, and lessons learnt from my early teaching experience to design a creative programme and a reasonable corresponding budget.

The final presentation was well received, and as a result, I was asked to conduct this Teacher Training Programme for two consecutive years.

For the duration of the six-week programme, at the end of each week, I was required to do a report on each volunteer. The psychologist assigned to work with me was also required to do a psychological report on each volunteer.

At the end of the six-week period, the psychologist told me that he was pleasantly surprised to find that for someone who was not schooled in psychology, the findings contained in my reports were similar to his. He further suggested that I should think seriously about graduate studies in psychometrics.

With this observation, he planted a seed in my mind, and thereon, my interest in measurement and evaluation began to take root and grow into what was to become for me an area of serious study and professional specialization.

I returned to Jamaica after the six-week training program was completed and worked with the Peace Corp volunteers in schools across the island in the teaching of mathematics. This I did until there came another turning point in my life.

Together with another young MOE officer, Eric Budhlall, we were selected as the two persons who were earmarked to occupy senior leadership positions in the MOE.

We would be assigned to be a part of the Inner Management Group, which included the permanent secretary, chief education officer, and chief planner, who worked directly with Education Minister Florizel Glasspole and Minister of State Eli Matalon.

At first I was very upset when I heard about this pending reassignment. I was thoroughly enjoying my work on the National Mathematics Project, and I felt professionally and personally fulfilled.

Working with the mathematics project required me to visit the ministry only twice per month—at the beginning of the month to present my monthly work schedule to Mr. Euclid King, and at the end of the month to hand in my monthly report and collect my salary and travel allowance.

I operated primarily from home and had a great time travelling to schools island-wide across the fourteen parishes of Jamaica.

In those days, we visited schools as a synergistic team of professionals with a diverse and dynamic combined skills set—mathematics, me and Moss-Solomon; music, Ouida Tomlinson and Lloyd Hall; dance, Sheila Barnett; and English, Keith Lowe.

This was the beginning of my understanding of the significant value and impact of *teamwork* on the education system.

Servant Leadership Lesson

It is important to have a network of human resource support groups in order to implement leadership initiatives effectively.

The schools we visited included the junior secondary schools that were just coming on stream under the New Deal for Education, spearheaded by Edwin Allen, the first minister of education in another political party's government administration, with whom I worked.

One Monday morning, I came in to see a memo on my desk.

My desk was located in an open area, dubbed the "bullpen," where several other officers and I worked. These officers included those whom I mentioned before, who were part of the "team visits" to schools.

Other officers in the bullpen included Ivy Cooke (who later became Lady Cooke when her husband, Sir Howard Cooke, an outstanding Miconian and former minister of education, was appointed governor general); Andrew Dunbar in agriculture; Franklyn Johnson (Rhodes Scholar); and Delroy Creary (brilliant school principal).

The memo read, "Report to the Permanent Secretary (PS) since you will now be in Room 304 as part of the Inner Management Group, with immediate effect."

I was depressed for days.

The permanent secretary, Pat Burke, sought to encourage me to shift my perspective and see the appointment as a positive opportunity. He indicated to me that this would provide me with invaluable experiences and lessons that I would not learn at any university.

Looking back, I thank him for his vision and his insight because this appointment turned out to be a game-changing experience in my management and leadership journey.

Through this experience, I learnt yet another vital leadership lesson.

Servant Leadership Lesson

It is important as a servant leader to provide persons you serve with opportunities for empowerment and upward mobility.

I had a rocky start working with the new minister of education, Florizel Glasspole.

I was working late one evening when he asked me to read a document, which I later found out was called a cabinet submission.

Being young and brash, and devoid of any diplomatic sensibility, I was forthright in conveying my response to him which in essence meant that that it "sounded like rubbish!"

He was not amused with my response. He did not speak with me for about two weeks.

To my great surprise, however, at the end of the agonizing two weeks, he assigned me, from thereon, to vet all of his cabinet submissions.

Eric Budhlall and I were also assigned to be available on the phone, in order to provide the minister with answers to questions raised in parliamentary committee meetings.

So I was forced to keep in my head, and have ready at my fingertips, a range of information, such as number of schools built or refurbished, how much was spent on the schools' nutrition program in a fiscal year, how many primary school students got high school places based on their performance on the Common Entrance Examination, etc.

With respect to the latter information (the number of primary school students who got high school places…), the previous minister of education, Edwin Allen, had established the 70:30 ratio for placement, i.e., 70 percent of the students placed in high schools from the Common Entrance Examination results should be from primary schools and 30 percent from preparatory schools.

Looking back, I did not know that my honest, though decidedly audacious, "rubbish" comment had opened up an amazing portal through which I could explore the powerful and amazing realm of transformational leadership.

The term "transformational leadership" was first coined about 1973 or so by renowned sociologist James V. Downton and further developed by leadership expert James MacGregor Burns.

Later, around 1985, researcher Bernard M. Bass expanded the concept to include ways for measuring the success of transformational leadership.

According to Bass, the hallmarks of a transformational leader are someone who

- encourages the motivation and positive development of followers;

- exemplifies moral standards within the organization and encourages the same of others;

- fosters an ethical work environment with clear values, priorities, and standards;

- builds company culture by encouraging employees to move from an attitude of self-interest to a mindset where they are working for the common good;

- holds an emphasis on authenticity, cooperation, and open communication; and

- provides coaching and mentoring but allows employees to make decisions and take ownership of tasks.

The then minister of education, Florizel Glasspole, by entrusting me with the great responsibility to vet all of his cabinet submissions, even after I had "rubbished" his early draft, exemplified all of Bass's key characteristics of a transformational leader as outlined above.

According to the Greek philosopher Aristotle, "To be a leader, he has to be a follower."

The minister, as a transformational leader, both influenced and strengthened my capacity to model that Aristotle-style leadership and, in years to come, gave me a distinct leadership advantage in all the arenas in which my leadership was applied.

Essentially, as Wikipedia so succinctly puts it, transformational leadership "is a theory of leadership where a leader works with teams to identify needed change, creating a vision to guide the change through inspiration, and executing the change in tandem with committed members of a group."

Referencing Sarah K. White, senior writer, CIO, transformational leadership is a "leadership style in which leaders encourage, inspire and motivate employees to innovate and create change that will help grow and shape the future success of the company."

White also writes that transformational leaders "inspire and motivate their workforce without micromanaging—they trust trained employees to take authority over decisions in their assigned jobs. It's a management style that's designed to give employees more room to be creative, look to the future and find new solutions to old problems."

I learnt several profound truths throughout the course of my early work-life journey. Several of those truths have been seared into my consciousness, one of which follows:

Servant Leadership Lesson

Creativity and brilliance are distributed across all communities of people. Being poor does not mean that you live in poverty. Real wealth lies in the use of the gifts and talents, the will to succeed, channeled through creativity, innovation, self-confidence, positive outlook on life, and resilience.

From a leadership perspective, two other truths that are indelibly imprinted in my mind based on my early work-life experiences and which I encourage you to embrace and demonstrate are these:

> Leadership is not about titles, positions or flow charts. It is about one life influencing another.—John C. Maxwell

> Leaders instill in their people a hope for success and a belief in themselves. Positive leaders empower people to accomplish their goals.—Unknown

8

The Servant Leader Ready for Service:
Lessons Learnt, Competencies Acquired, Insights Gained

DURING THE PROCESS of being shaped as a servant leader, I have learnt important lessons, acquired useful leadership competencies, and gleaned important insights. These were the results of my life experiences and exposures from early childhood, boyhood, and schools (elementary to college and universities), early job assignments, and in-between and beyond…complete with the diverse mix of people and events that have impacted my world.

Altogether, I have been moulded and shaped and "fired at the kiln" in readiness to serve people and organizations and add transformational value as a servant leader.

In charting the course of my servant leadership journey, I have developed a Servant Leadership Framework for Action involving three components: Lessons Learnt, Competencies Acquired, and Insights Gained.

In the sections that follow, I will share with you the details and features of these components.

Servant Leadership Lessons Learnt

I have classified the servant leadership lessons I have learnt in three major clusters to form the action framework for being an effective servant leader.

Cluster 1: Guiding Philosophy for Servant Leadership

Cluster 2: Building and Nurturing Relationships with People

Cluster 3: Developing and Using a Servant Leadership Toolkit for Action

- **Guiding Philosophy for Servant Leadership**

The journey of servant leadership has its joys but also its challenges.

There are times when there are no clear pathways or rules, but the servant leader must continue the journey regardless, guided only by a commitment to the compelling mission of service to others.

In continuing this journey, keep reminding yourself of these truths:

The greatest gift God gave to you is your brain. Use it wisely and use it well to improve the quality of your life, but more importantly, use it to improve the quality of life of others.

This statement of truth forms the philosophical mantra that serves as a compass to guide, as well as strengthen and motivate, me to continue, unswervingly, with steadfast purpose on the journey of serving others.

- **Building and Nurturing Relationships with People**

The relationship you build with others creates a portal through which you are allowed to enter and be received into their personal space, thereby enabling you to serve them effectively.

- **Developing and Using a Servant Leadership Toolkit for Action**

Servant leadership requires taking specific actions in order to have the desired impact you intend to have on the people you serve. It is the vehicle for converting laudable intentions into actual service to others.

I will now share with you my summary of the servant leadership lessons I have learnt under these three major clusters.

1: GUIDING PHILOSOPHY FOR SERVANT LEADERSHIP

- **Have a clear and compelling mission for service.**

Helping others to achieve their true potential is your most important mission in life.

A servant leader is one whose priority intention is empowering others to have the capacity and passion to improve the quality of their lives.

- **Use your talents to serve others.**

I have said it before, but it bears repeating; it is that important.

The greatest gift God gave to you is your brain. Use it wisely and use it well to improve the quality of your life, but more importantly, use it to improve the quality of life of others.

- **Avoid biases when serving others.**

As a servant leader do not make assumptions about the talents of those you serve based on your biases relating to the communities in which they are born and raised.

Creativity and brilliance are distributed across all communities of people. Encourage people you serve to realize that being poor does not mean that you live in poverty.

- **Focus on knowing and understanding persons you serve.**

Spend time getting to know those you serve in both formal and informal settings and situations.

Understanding the needs, challenges, and concerns of persons you serve provides an important platform for demonstrating genuine care for them.

- **Focus on self-reliance.**

Servant leadership must involve the objective of self-reliance as a key building block for empowering the persons being served.

It is important as a servant leader to provide people you serve with opportunities for empowerment and upward mobility.

- **Convert difficulties into creative ideas and innovative actions.**

Use difficulties you experience in life to motivate you to develop and implement creative and innovative solutions.

2: BUILDING AND NURTURING RELATIONSHIPS WITH PEOPLE

- **Build lasting bonds of trust.**

True and solid relationships play a key role in making your servant leadership successful.

Establishing trust with those you serve is the most important element in the process of building effective relationships. The servant leader should therefore focus on nurturing lasting bonds of trust.

Trust is a unity of hearts, minds, and souls with persons whom you serve. Treasure that trust and strive continuously to keep that bond of trust intact.

Present your authentic self.

Always show up with your authentic self and present who you really are. Be genuine.

It is of vital importance to let others know the "real you." Fakes are easily detected and dishonoured.

Let those whom you lead, know where you stand on issues. Be open and honest. Dealing straightforwardly with others is the key to being an authentic servant leader.

- **Display ethical behaviours.**

Honesty and transparency are important at all times, especially when your leadership decision is unpopular and out of favour with those whom you lead and serve.

Display transparency, integrity, and fair play in your decision-making.

- **Display sensitivity and respect in relation to sociocultural realities of persons you serve.**

You should invest time in knowing, understanding, and appreciating, without judgement or bias, the varying cultures of people you serve and the environment in which you and they operate.

- **Display caring when serving others.**

Show empathy to persons in need.

Spiritual and psychological support is very important in our relationships with persons we serve, especially when they are experiencing hardships and difficulties.

Spending quality time to help people deal with their problems is good therapy for both them and you.

When you are nurturing and assisting others, focus on developing a relationship with them that conveys you genuinely care about them as individuals. This is more important than your financial support if you are going to make a positive difference in their lives.

- **Develop friendships that are mutually beneficial.**

Unquestionably, as I have come to know from experience, friends and friendships are two of the most valuable tools in our life's toolkit.

Leadership is all about relationships. The connections we make and cultivate and the friendships we create and nurture along our life's journey can enrich the quality of our leadership and service to others.

Solid friendships formed earlier in life can play a significant role later in life to facilitate success of your leadership initiatives.

- **Be careful about the influence of the halo effect.**

Be careful about how your overall impression of persons you serve impacts your evaluation of their behaviour and use of their talents.

3: DEVELOPING AND USING A SERVANT LEADERSHIP TOOLKIT FOR ACTION

- **Engage in holistic education.**

Holistic education is an effective model for preparing yourself and those you serve to develop and practice servant leadership.

Cultural activities and sports are important influencers in your development and functioning as a servant leader.

It is important to acquire and utilize social graces in the process of leadership development.

- **Be brave and move out of your comfort zone.**

To be successful in attempting transformative initiatives as a servant leader, there are critical points of time in your life when you have to be brave and come out of your comfort zone, and do things you have never done before.

Visioning is important to enable those you serve to visualize future possibilities for their progress and success.

- **Use critical turning points in your life to plot new directions.**

Use critical turning points in your life to explore new possibilities for future success and encourage those you serve to do the same.

- **Inspire people you serve.**

Motivate those you serve to focus on a brighter future instead of their present circumstances.

- **Build a supportive professional network.**

Develop useful and mutually beneficial professional networks to support and facilitate the implementation of your servant leadership initiatives.

Emphasize *knowledge sharing* and *collaboration* in this process.

It is important to listen to and accommodate radically different ideas and viewpoints.

- **Focus on cultural adaptability.**

Cultural adaptability is important to be an effective leader in both a national as well as in an international context.

Practice to live and work harmoniously with people from different cultures while preserving your unique identity.

- **Challenge and transform.**

As a servant leader, challenge the status quo and existing paradigms, but at the same time, come up with creative ideas and innovative actions that can positively transform what you are challenging.

- **Be a mentor.**

Mentorship is an important part of your role as a servant leader in building the self-esteem and self-confidence of the people you serve.

- **Have fun while serving others.**

Use humour to help you enjoy serving others as well as to help them enjoy your service.

- **Work with others to achieve a common goal.**

When performing your servant leadership roles, give focused attention to teamwork and collaboration among the persons you serve.

Collaboration and teamwork benefit the servant leader as well as those being served.

It is important as a servant leader to differentiate between your role and the role of others and to recognize the value of the combination of these roles.

- **Practice time management.**

Time management is important in balancing job responsibilities and voluntary services while seeking to empower the people you serve.

When we appreciate the value and importance of time, and develop the skills to apply it, manage it, and optimize it, time will be truly well spent.

- **Develop and use negotiation skills.**

It is important as a servant leader that you develop and use the art and science of negotiation to resolve both intrapersonal as well as interpersonal conflicts.

- **Practice lifelong learning.**

Learn continuously from a variety of situations—formal and conventional, as well as informal and unconventional.

As a servant leader it is important that you continuously learn and demonstrate that you value the importance of preparation research and the continuous renewing and refreshing of your knowledge.

SERVANT LEADERSHIP COMPETENCIES

The acquisition and use of strategic thinking, emotional intelligence competencies, and conversational competencies are of critical importance in your development and practice as a servant leader.

You must be alert to the fact that these can be acquired and/or developed through conventional, formal educational settings, as well as informal, unconventional settings.

The bottom line is that it is the accumulation of life experiences, formal and informal education, and training that shape each of us to be an effective servant leader.

During the journey that shaped me as a servant leader, I acquired three important servant leadership competencies—strategic thinking, conversational competencies, and emotional intelligence competencies—which I will utilize in my future role as a servant leader.

In my acquisition of these servant leadership competencies, I combined my experiences and practices with the views of thought leaders and researchers.

Strategic Thinking

This process involves formulating different scenarios for success for today and tomorrow, as well as how to inspire the persons I serve to plan for the future, while simultaneously responding to their present realities. In this process, creativity and innovation are important areas of focus while empowering those I serve so they can grasp current and future opportunities for upward social and economic mobility.

During my servant leadership development journey, I learnt that strategic thinking is of critical importance when we have to respond to and plan for the effects of major events that disrupt our lives and the economies and environment of the countries in which we live.

Here are three poignant examples of these disruptive events:

1. Pandemics such as COVID-19, which is currently uppermost in our minds

2. Natural disasters, such as hurricanes, earthquakes, and tsunamis, resulting from the effects of global warming and climate change

3. New and emerging technologies such as artificial intelligence and big data, which are leading us into the fourth Industrial Revolution

Emotional Intelligence Competencies

In the area of emotional intelligence (EI) and emotional intelligence competencies (EIC), I found very useful the work and views of Daniel Goleman and Richard Boyatzis (2017), Ronald Riggio (2014), and Matthew Schieltz and Michel Seidel (2019). Two of these areas of value to me are

1. The four domains of EI, namely self awareness, self-management, social awareness, and relationship building.

2. Four important elements of EI and EIC on which the servant leader should focus:

- **Idealized Influence of Leaders**

    Idealized influence involves the leader building trust with his/her followers and the followers, in turn, developing confidence in their leader.

- **Inspirational Motivation**

    Inspirational motivation refers to the leader's ability to inspire confidence, a sense of purpose, and excitement and commitment for action in his followers.

- **Intellectual Stimulation**

    Intellectual stimulation involves the leader placing great value on creativity and autonomy among the followers and challenging followers to display higher levels of critical thinking.

- **Individualized Consideration**

    Individualized consideration involves the leader demonstrating genuine concern for the needs and feelings of followers.

The following are three of the important practical aspects of emotional intelligence competencies that I acquired:

- Inspiring and motivating the people I serve

- Empathizing with the fears, concerns, and needs of those I serve

- Building self-confidence and capacity for self-reliance in those I serve

Conversational Competencies

The Newfield Network did some interesting and useful work in this area, and one of their writers, Richard LeKander (2015), made contextual points related to organizations which I found useful in trying to understand and implement conversational competencies.

Two of these points are as follows:

1. Organizations in general and business organizations in particular are linguistic phenomena: units built from specific conversations and based on the capacity human beings have to make declarations and mutual commitments with each other.

2. When people participate in this tapestry of conversations, their personal identities become intertwined with the identity of the organization. We call this tapestry of personal/organizational identity the organization's culture.

The following are two of the important practical dimensions of conversational competencies that I acquired:

- Using compelling conversations to inspire persons to move out of their comfort zone and try things they have never done before.

- Communicating with clarity and conviction so the persons I serve understand what I am saying. And most importantly, that they become excited to buy into the vision for transformational changes I am inviting them to share, and be motivated to join me in the journey to realize this vision.

SERVANT LEADERSHIP INSIGHTS

During my journey of becoming a servant leader, I gained certain insights—some of which are little known and recognized—that have assisted me in having a better understanding of my purpose as a servant leader.

I have used the insights I have gleaned to assist me in answering a fundamental question that prompted me to write this book:

Should leaders focus on their power and authority, and their own personal growth, development, and progress, or on the empowerment of the persons they serve?

The answer to this question is encapsulated in the insights I will share with you, which have enabled me to determine the purpose of my servant leadership.

You have to remind yourself continuously that servant leadership is about mutual benefits.

Your servant leadership efforts should improve the quality of your life, but more importantly, they must improve the quality of life for those you serve

In order to truly be a servant leader, this principle of *mutuality* must be the compass that guides your leadership actions.

I am thankful for the episodes and experiences in my life and the persons who played a significant role in shaping me to be a servant leader. They have helped me to achieve this balance, required by the principle of mutuality, both in my substantive professional career and in voluntary services.

I have learnt important lessons in my servant leadership development journey. These lessons have reinforced in my mind the duality of the real purpose of servant leadership, which is the empowerment of self-simultaneous with the empowerment of the persons we serve.

The synergistic effect of each of us achieving this duality of purpose is what will contribute meaningfully to the world being a better place for all of us.

This duality of purpose, when achieved, is the vehicle that transports the servant leader to the arena of transformational leadership.

In this arena the servant leader influences radical changes toward creating positive mindsets and positive actions. These outcomes take the people we serve to new and exciting destinations.

In this transformative process, hope, creative ideas, and innovative actions replace fear, despair, and the mental restrictions generated by the hurdles and difficulties in the pathway of life.

This is the essence of the value of the empowerment initiatives of a servant leader. This type of empowerment provides the people we serve with the launching pad to soar with the vision of a brighter future, with possibilities for the realization of success and happiness.

Conclusion:
Shaping a Servant Leader: A Continuous Process

> A story really isn't truly a story
> until it reaches its climax and conclusion.
> —Ted Naifeh

SHAPING A SERVANT leader is a continuous leadership development process. During this process the servant leader is immersed in learning, doing, reflecting, analyzing, evaluating, creating, inspiring, caring, growing, and evolving.

The major outcome of this immersion is the increased transformative value of the servant leader to the people and organizations being served.

There are some important events in this continuous leadership development process that are important to note.

The Servant Leader

- Learning lessons, acquiring competencies, and gleaning insights

- Developing a servant leadership toolkit for action

- Implementing the action toolkit for transforming people and organizations being served

- Utilizing opportunities to hone servant leadership competencies

- Reimagining new possibilities for transformational initiatives and changes

During this continuous leadership development process, the servant leader must give focused attention to the compelling mission of servant leadership.

A servant leader is one whose priority intention is empowering others to have the capacity and passion to improve the quality of their lives.

In the foregoing chapters, I have shared with you stories, lessons, insights, skills, and competencies that I have acquired on my continuous servant leadership development journey. These have shaped me and continue to shape me to be a more effective servant leader.

I trust that in reading this book, you have found some useful servant leadership nuggets. My hope is that you will be inspired to use them to add positive value to your life and to the lives of people with whom you interact and serve.

Servant leadership has served me well in both my personal and professional life. Even more so, it has served countless others in the multifaceted areas of their lives. My passion to serve others is unbridled and never-ending.

My faith and my principles lead me always to travel the broad and scenic highway of service to others and eschew the narrow trail of self-interest.

I urge you to…

Make servant leadership a relationship that is exciting, productive, enjoyable, and beneficial for both you and those you serve.

The discussion on servant leadership has not concluded; my servant leadership journey continues. I am still growing, still learning, still serving, and still evolving as a servant leader.

I never tire of thinking or exploring new thoughts and ideas, or of shifting and sometimes outright debunking some of my old concepts and ways of being, in favour of those that are new and relevant.

I will continue the important role of being a servant leader guided by my mantra:

The relationship you build with others creates a portal through which you are allowed to enter and be received into their personal space, thereby enabling you to serve them effectively.

CPSIA information can be obtained
at www.ICGtesting.com
Printed in the USA
LVHW081415290521
688880LV00002B/257